HEALING FOODS OF THE BIBLE

Divine Nutrition for Body and Soul

Dr. Maxwell Shimba

Printed in the United States of America

TABLE OF CONTENTS

INTRODUCTION

Food has always been a cornerstone of human existence, playing a crucial role in the survival, culture, and health of societies throughout history. In ancient cultures, food was not only a source of nourishment but also a symbol of community, spirituality, and healing. The Bible, one of the oldest and most influential texts in human history, provides a rich tapestry of references to food, highlighting its significance in the lives of its characters and followers.

Overview of the Importance of Food in Ancient Cultures

In ancient times, food was more than just sustenance. It was deeply embedded in the social, religious, and economic fabric of life. Agricultural practices dictated the rhythms of the year, with planting and harvest seasons marking important communal activities. Festivals and religious observances often centered around food, celebrating the bounty of the earth and honoring the gods or God who provided it.

In many ancient cultures, including those depicted in the Bible, food was a sign of hospitality and a means of establishing and strengthening relationships. Sharing a meal was a sacred act, fostering a sense of community and mutual respect. For instance, Abraham's hospitality to the three visitors in Genesis 18 exemplifies the importance of food in forging bonds and showing reverence to guests.

Food also played a crucial role in rituals and offerings. In the Bible, sacrifices often included grains, wine, and animals, symbolizing devotion and thanksgiving to God. The Passover meal, as described in Exodus, is a poignant example of how food commemorated significant historical and spiritual events, reinforcing collective memory and identity.

Introduction to the Concept of Healing Through Food in the Bible

The Bible is replete with references to the healing properties of food. From the manna that sustained the Israelites in the wilderness to the figs used by Hezekiah to cure his boils, the Scriptures highlight a profound understanding of food as a source of physical and spiritual healing.

The concept of healing through food is intertwined with the belief in God as the ultimate healer. In Exodus 15:26, God declares, "I am the Lord who heals you." This divine assurance extends to the provision of food that not only sustains but also heals. The dietary laws given to the Israelites in Leviticus reflect an awareness of health and well-being, promoting foods that contribute to vitality and avoiding those that could cause harm.

Foods like honey, olive oil, and herbs such as hyssop are frequently mentioned in the Bible for their medicinal qualities. Honey is noted for its sweetness and health benefits, often symbolizing abundance and pleasure (Proverbs 24:13). Olive oil, a staple in the Mediterranean diet, is used for anointing and healing wounds (Isaiah 1:6, Luke 10:34). Herbs like hyssop are associated with purification and healing, as seen in Psalm 51:7.

The New Testament continues this theme, with Jesus using food in his healing ministry. He miraculously feeds the multitudes with loaves and fishes, symbolizing spiritual and physical nourishment (Matthew 14:13-21). Jesus also institutes the Lord's Supper, using bread and wine to signify his body and blood, thus providing profound spiritual sustenance and healing.

Bridging Ancient Wisdom and Modern Understanding

The biblical perspective on food as a source of healing resonates with modern nutritional science, which recognizes the importance of diet in maintaining health and preventing disease. Foods mentioned in the Bible, such as whole grains, fruits, vegetables, and fish, are celebrated today for their health benefits.

By exploring the healing foods of the Bible, we not only gain insight into the dietary practices of ancient peoples but also discover timeless principles that can enhance our health and well-being today. This book will delve into the specific foods mentioned in the Bible, examining their historical context, nutritional value, and potential health benefits.

As we embark on this journey, let us open our hearts and minds to the wisdom of the Scriptures, appreciating the divine provision of food that heals, sustains, and nourishes both body and soul. Through this exploration, we hope to bridge the ancient and the modern, enriching our lives with the healing foods of the Bible.

PLANTS, VEGETABLES, FRUITS, AND FOODS MENTIONED

Here is a list of all the plants, vegetables, fruits, and foods mentioned in the book, along with their meanings and significance in the biblical context.

Plants, Vegetables, Fruits, and Foods Mentioned

1. Barley

- Meaning and Significance: Barley was a staple grain in the ancient Near East and is often associated with sustenance and provision. It was used in offerings and represented God's provision for His people.

2. Wheat

- Meaning and Significance: Wheat is another staple grain that symbolizes abundance, harvest, and God's blessing. It was also used in offerings and bread-making.

3. Figs

- Meaning and Significance: Figs are mentioned frequently in the Bible, symbolizing prosperity, peace, and well-being. They were used both as food and medicinally.

4. Grapes and Wine

- Meaning and Significance: Grapes and wine represent joy, blessing, and celebration. Wine is also symbolic of Jesus' blood in the New Covenant, representing sacrifice and salvation.

5. Pomegranates

- Meaning and Significance: Pomegranates symbolize fertility, abundance, and the beauty of God's creation. They were used in decoration and as a food source.

6. Olives and Olive Oil

- Meaning and Significance: Olives and olive oil are symbols of peace, anointing, and healing. Olive oil was used in rituals, cooking, and medicinal practices.

7. Honey

- Meaning and Significance: Honey represents sweetness, delight, and the abundance of the Promised Land. It was valued for its taste and healing properties.

8. Herbs and Spices (Hyssop, Mint, Dill, Cumin)

- Meaning and Significance:

- Hyssop: Symbolizes purification and cleansing. It was used in ritualistic practices.

- Mint, Dill, Cumin: These herbs and spices represent the detailed care and provision of God. They were used for flavoring food and had medicinal uses.

9. Mustard Seed

- Meaning and Significance: The mustard seed symbolizes faith and growth. Despite its small size, it grows into a large plant, illustrating the potential of even small acts of faith.

10. Lentils

- Meaning and Significance: Lentils are a symbol of nourishment and sustenance. They were a common food and provided essential nutrients.

11. Dates

- Meaning and Significance: Dates symbolize fertility and prosperity. They were a staple food and a source of natural sweetness.

12. Garlic

- Meaning and Significance: While not explicitly mentioned in the Bible, garlic was a staple in ancient diets. It symbolizes health and protection, known for its medicinal properties.

13. Cucumbers

- Meaning and Significance: Cucumbers are mentioned as part of the diet in Egypt, symbolizing refreshment and the desire for the familiar foods of the past.

14. Milk and Honey

- Meaning and Significance: Milk and honey together symbolize prosperity, abundance, and the fulfillment of God's promises. They are often used to describe the richness of the Promised Land.

15. Fish

- Meaning and Significance: Fish symbolize provision and sustenance. They were a staple food for many people living near water bodies and are also associated with several miracles performed by Jesus.

16. Bread

- Meaning and Significance: Bread represents life, sustenance, and provision. It is central to many biblical narratives, including the feeding of the multitudes and the Last Supper, symbolizing Jesus' body.

17. Balm of Gilead

- Meaning and Significance: The Balm of Gilead symbolizes healing and restoration. It was a valuable medicinal ointment known for its soothing properties.

Each of these foods carries rich symbolic meanings and practical significance in the Bible. They represent God's provision, the bounty of the land, and various spiritual truths such as faith, healing, and abundance. By understanding the biblical context of these foods, we can appreciate their deeper spiritual implications and their enduring relevance to our lives today.

xiii

DR. MAXWELL SHIMBA

CHAPTER 01

BIBLICAL PERSPECTIVE ON FOOD

Food is central to the narrative of the Bible, shaping the lives and practices of its characters from Genesis to Revelation. In both the Old and New Testaments, food serves not only as physical sustenance but also as a symbol of God's provision, a means of fellowship, and a conduit for spiritual lessons. This chapter explores the significance of food in biblical times, highlighting its role in religious rituals, social customs, and divine teachings.

Food in the Old Testament

Creation and Provision

The Bible opens with the creation story, where God provides the first humans with a bountiful diet. In Genesis 1:29, God says, "Behold, I have given you every herb bearing seed, which is upon the face of all the earth, and every tree, in the which is the fruit of a tree yielding seed; to you, it shall be for meat." This verse establishes food as a divine gift, intended to sustain and nourish humanity. The Garden of Eden is depicted as a paradise of abundance, where Adam and Eve have access to a variety of fruits and plants.

Dietary Laws and Cleanliness

As the narrative progresses, food continues to play a crucial role in the covenantal relationship between God and His people. The dietary laws given to the Israelites in Leviticus and Deuteronomy outline what is clean and unclean to eat. These laws, found in Leviticus 11 and Deuteronomy 14, are comprehensive, covering land animals, sea creatures, birds, and insects. The distinction between clean and unclean animals serves multiple purposes: it fosters obedience to God's commands, promotes health and hygiene, and sets the Israelites apart as a holy people.

For example, Leviticus 11:3-4 states, "Whatsoever parteth the hoof, and is cloven-footed, and cheweth the cud, among the beasts, that shall ye eat. Nevertheless, these shall ye not eat of them that chew the cud, or of them that divide the hoof: as the camel, because he cheweth the cud, but divideth not the hoof; he is unclean unto you." These regulations not only guided the Israelites' dietary practices but also reinforced their identity and commitment to God.

Feasts and Festivals

Food is integral to the religious feasts and festivals ordained by God. These events commemorate significant moments in Israel's history and celebrate God's provision and deliverance. The Passover, described in Exodus 12, is a prime example. The Passover meal, consisting of lamb, unleavened bread, and bitter herbs, memorializes the Israelites' escape from Egypt and God's protection during the final plague. Each element of the meal has symbolic meaning, reflecting aspects of the Exodus story and God's saving power.

Other notable feasts include the Feast of Unleavened Bread, the Feast of Weeks (Pentecost), the Feast of Trumpets, the Day of Atonement, and the Feast of Tabernacles. Each of these occasions involves specific foods and rituals that reinforce communal identity, gratitude, and worship. Leviticus 23 provides a detailed account of these festivals, emphasizing their importance in the spiritual life of the Israelites.

Stories of Provision and Sustenance

The Old Testament is replete with stories highlighting God's provision through food. One of the most notable is the manna from heaven. When the Israelites wander in the wilderness, God miraculously provides manna to sustain them. Exodus 16:4 records God's promise: "Then said the Lord unto Moses, Behold, I will rain bread from heaven for you; and the people shall go out and gather a certain rate every day, that I may prove them, whether they will walk in my law, or no." This daily provision of manna teaches the Israelites to trust in God's constant care and to rely on Him for their needs.

Another significant story is Elijah's sustenance by ravens and the widow of Zarephath. During a severe drought, God commands ravens to bring Elijah bread and meat (1 Kings 17:6). Later, God directs Elijah to a widow who, despite her meager resources, provides him with food, and in return, her supply of flour and oil does not run out (1 Kings 17:14-16). These stories exemplify God's miraculous provision and the theme of divine hospitality.

Food in the New Testament

Jesus and Food

In the New Testament, food continues to hold deep symbolic and practical significance. Jesus frequently uses food in His teachings and miracles. One of His most famous miracles is the feeding of the 5,000, recorded in all four Gospels (Matthew 14:13-21, Mark 6:30-44, Luke 9:10-17, John 6:1-14). With five loaves and two fish, Jesus feeds a multitude, demonstrating His compassion and divine power. This miracle not only meets the physical needs of the crowd but also serves as a sign of Jesus' identity as the Bread of Life (John 6:35).

The Last Supper is another pivotal moment where Jesus uses food to convey profound spiritual truths. During this meal, Jesus institutes the Eucharist, breaking bread and sharing wine with His disciples as symbols of His body and blood. Luke 22:19-20 records Jesus' words: "And he took bread, and gave thanks, and brake it, and gave unto them, saying, This is my body which is given for you: this do in remembrance of me. Likewise, also the cup after supper, saying, This cup is the new testament in my blood, which is shed for you." This act establishes a central rite for Christian worship and underscores the sacrificial nature of Jesus' mission.

Early Christian Practices

In the early Christian community, food continues to be a means of fellowship and worship. The communal meals, or agape feasts, mentioned in Jude 1:12 and 1 Corinthians 11:20-22, are occasions for believers to gather, share food, and celebrate their faith. These meals emphasize the values of equality, generosity, and unity within the body of Christ.

The apostle Paul also addresses dietary concerns in his letters, advising believers on issues of food sacrificed to idols and the exercise of personal freedom. In 1 Corinthians 8 and

Romans 14, Paul emphasizes that while Christians have the liberty to eat various foods, they should be mindful of the impact on others and prioritize love and edification within the community.

Symbolism and Revelation

Food symbolism extends into the book of Revelation, where the marriage supper of the Lamb (Revelation 19:9) symbolizes the ultimate union between Christ and His Church. The imagery of a feast reflects the culmination of God's redemptive plan and the eternal joy and fellowship believers will experience in His presence.

The biblical perspective on food encompasses physical sustenance, spiritual symbolism, and divine provision. From the Old Testament laws and festivals to the New Testament teachings and miracles, food is a recurring theme that illustrates God's care for His people and His desire for their well-being. By understanding the significance of food in the Bible, we gain insights into the holistic nature of God's provision, which nurtures both body and soul. As we explore the healing foods of the Bible in subsequent chapters, we will uncover the timeless wisdom that continues to nourish and heal us today.

Dietary Laws and Guidelines in the Bible (Kosher Laws, Clean and Unclean Foods)

The dietary laws and guidelines presented in the Bible, particularly in the books of Leviticus and Deuteronomy, are fundamental to understanding the biblical perspective on food. These laws, commonly known as kosher laws, dictate what is considered clean and unclean, permissible and forbidden, for consumption by the Israelites. These regulations were not only about health and hygiene but also about obedience to God and maintaining a distinct identity as His chosen people.

The Foundation of Dietary Laws

The foundation of dietary laws is laid out in the Torah, the first five books of the Bible. In particular, Leviticus 11 and Deuteronomy 14 provide detailed lists of animals that are considered clean and unclean. The primary purpose of these laws was to set the Israelites apart from other nations, fostering holiness and dedication to God.

In Leviticus 11:44-45, God commands, "For I am the Lord your God: ye shall therefore sanctify yourselves, and ye shall be holy; for I am holy: neither shall ye defile yourselves with any manner of creeping thing that creepeth upon the earth. For I am the Lord that bringeth you up out of the land of Egypt, to be your God: ye shall therefore be holy, for I am holy." This call to holiness underpins the dietary regulations, emphasizing the need for purity and separation from defilement.

Clean and Unclean Animals

The distinction between clean and unclean animals is a central aspect of the kosher laws. Leviticus 11 and Deuteronomy 14 categorize animals based on their physical characteristics and behaviors.

Land Animals:

Clean animals are those that have a split hoof and chew the cud. Examples include cattle, sheep, and goats. Unclean animals, which do not meet both criteria, include pigs, camels, and rabbits. Leviticus 11:3-4 states, "Whatsoever parteth the hoof, and is cloven-footed, and cheweth the cud, among the beasts, that shall ye eat. Nevertheless, these shall ye not eat of them that chew the cud, or of them that divide the hoof: as the camel, because he cheweth the cud, but divideth not the hoof; he is unclean unto you."

Sea Creatures:

Clean sea creatures are those with fins and scales, such as fish like salmon and cod. Creatures without fins and scales, such as shellfish, eels, and catfish, are considered unclean. Leviticus 11:9-10 specifies, "These shall ye eat of all that are in the waters: whatsoever hath fins and scales in the waters, in the seas, and in the rivers, them shall ye eat. And all that have not fins and scales in the seas, and in the rivers, of all that move in the waters, and of any living thing which is in the waters, they shall be an abomination unto you."

Birds:

The Bible lists specific birds that are considered unclean, including birds of prey and scavengers like eagles, vultures, and ravens. Clean birds, which are generally domesticated species, include chickens, doves, and quail. Leviticus 11:13-19 provides a list of unclean birds, such as "the eagle, and the ossifrage, and the ospray, and the vulture, and the kite after his kind; every raven after his kind."

Insects:

Among insects, those that have jointed legs for hopping, such as locusts, crickets, and grasshoppers, are considered clean. Other insects, particularly those that crawl or fly without hopping, are deemed unclean. Leviticus 11:22-23 states, "Even these of them ye may eat; the locust after his kind, and the bald locust after his kind, and the beetle after his kind, and the grasshopper after his kind. But all other flying creeping things, which have four feet, shall be an abomination unto you."

Reasons for Dietary Laws

The dietary laws served multiple purposes, encompassing health, spiritual discipline, and cultural identity.

Health and Hygiene:

Some scholars believe that the dietary laws had practical health benefits, protecting the Israelites from consuming animals that were more likely to carry diseases or parasites. For example, pigs are known to be carriers of trichinosis, a parasitic disease that can be transmitted to humans through undercooked pork. By prohibiting the consumption of pork, the Israelites were safeguarded against this health risk.

Spiritual Discipline:

Adhering to dietary laws required constant mindfulness and discipline, reinforcing a daily practice of obedience to God. Every meal became an opportunity to affirm one's commitment to God's commandments. This discipline helped cultivate a sense of holiness and separation from worldly influences.

Cultural Identity:

The dietary laws also functioned as a marker of cultural and religious identity. By following these unique dietary practices, the Israelites distinguished themselves from surrounding nations, reinforcing their status as God's chosen people. This separation was essential for maintaining their cultural and religious integrity, especially during periods of exile and interaction with other cultures.

The New Testament Perspective

The New Testament brings a shift in the understanding of dietary laws, reflecting the new covenant established through Jesus Christ. While the early Christian community grappled with the relevance of kosher laws, the teachings of Jesus and the apostles ultimately emphasized spiritual purity over ritualistic adherence to dietary regulations.

Jesus' Teachings:

In Mark 7:18-19, Jesus challenges the traditional understanding of dietary laws, teaching that it is not what enters the body that defiles a person, but what comes out of the heart. He states, "Are ye so without understanding also? Do ye not perceive, that whatsoever thing from without entereth into the man, it cannot defile him; because it entereth not into his heart, but into the belly, and goeth out into the draught, purging all meats?" This teaching underscores the importance of inner purity and righteousness over external observances.

Peter's Vision:

The apostle Peter receives a vision that further transforms the understanding of clean and unclean foods. In Acts 10, Peter sees a sheet descending from heaven, filled with all kinds of animals, both clean and unclean. A voice instructs him, "Rise, Peter; kill, and eat." Peter initially resists, citing the dietary laws, but the voice responds, "What God hath cleansed, that call not thou common." This vision signifies the removal of dietary restrictions and the inclusion of Gentiles into the faith, emphasizing that God's grace extends beyond traditional boundaries.

Paul's Teachings:

The apostle Paul also addresses dietary issues in his letters, advocating for freedom and sensitivity within the Christian community. In Romans 14:14, he writes, "I know, and am persuaded by the Lord Jesus, that there is nothing unclean of itself: but to him that esteemeth anything to be unclean, to him it is unclean." Paul encourages believers to respect each other's dietary choices and to prioritize love and unity over dietary disputes.

The dietary laws and guidelines in the Bible reflect a profound intersection of health, spiritual discipline, and cultural identity. While the Old Testament emphasizes the importance of adhering to these laws as a means of holiness and obedience, the New Testament shifts the focus to inner purity and the universality of God's grace. Understanding these dietary principles provides valuable insights into the holistic nature of biblical teachings, which encompass both physical and spiritual well-being. As we explore further, we will uncover the timeless wisdom embedded in these ancient guidelines and their relevance to our lives today.

13

CHAPTER 02

HEALING FOODS IN THE OLD TESTAMENT

The Old Testament of the Bible is a rich source of knowledge about the foods that were considered not only nourishing but also healing. These foods, often used in conjunction with other practices, provided physical and spiritual benefits to the people of ancient Israel. This chapter delves into specific foods mentioned in the Old Testament for their healing purposes, exploring their historical context, uses, and the benefits they provided.

Honey

Honey is one of the most frequently mentioned healing foods in the Bible. It is noted for its sweetness and its health benefits. Proverbs 24:13 states, "My son, eat thou honey because it is good; and the honeycomb, which is sweet to thy taste." Honey was valued not only for its taste but also for its medicinal properties.

Historical Context and Uses:

In ancient times, honey was used as a natural sweetener, a preservative, and a medicine. Its antimicrobial properties make it a valuable resource for treating wounds and preventing infections. Honey was often applied to cuts and sores to promote healing and was also used to soothe sore throats and coughs.

Benefits:

Modern science has confirmed many of the health benefits of honey. It has antibacterial and anti-inflammatory properties, which can aid in wound healing and reduce inflammation. Honey also contains antioxidants that help protect the body from damage by free radicals.

Olive Oil

Olive oil is another significant healing food mentioned in the Old Testament. It was used for anointing, cooking, and as a base for various medicinal preparations. In Isaiah 1:6, the use of oil for healing is highlighted: "From the sole of the foot even unto the head there is no soundness in it; but wounds, and bruises, and putrifying sores: they have not been closed, neither bound up, neither mollified with ointment."

Historical Context and Uses:

Olive oil was a staple in the Mediterranean diet and was used in religious ceremonies, including anointing kings and priests. It was also used in lamps for lighting. Medicinally, olive oil was used as a base for salves and ointments to treat wounds and skin conditions.

Benefits:

Olive oil is rich in monounsaturated fats and antioxidants, which promote heart health and reduce inflammation. It is also beneficial for skin health, helping to moisturize and protect the skin. Studies have shown that olive oil can aid in wound healing and improve the overall health of the skin.

Figs

Figs are mentioned in the Bible as a healing food, particularly in the story of King Hezekiah's illness. In 2 Kings 20:7, the prophet Isaiah prescribes a fig poultice to heal Hezekiah's boil: "And Isaiah said, Take a lump of figs. And they took and laid it on the boil, and he recovered."

Historical Context and Uses:

Figs were a common fruit in the ancient Near East, eaten fresh or dried. They were also used medicinally, as demonstrated in Hezekiah's healing. Fig poultices were used to treat various ailments, including boils and skin infections.

Benefits:

Figs are rich in fiber, vitamins, and minerals, including potassium, calcium, and magnesium. They have been found to promote digestive health, reduce inflammation, and improve blood sugar levels. The use of figs in poultices can be attributed to their natural enzymes and bioactive compounds that aid in healing and reduce inflammation.

Grapes and Wine

Grapes and their byproduct, wine, are frequently mentioned in the Bible for their health benefits. In 1 Timothy 5:23, Paul advises Timothy, "Drink no longer water but use a little wine for thy stomach's sake and thine often infirmities."

Historical Context and Uses:

Grapes were cultivated widely in ancient Israel and were consumed fresh, dried as raisins, or fermented into wine. Wine was used not only as a beverage but also for its medicinal properties. It was often mixed with water to purify it and was used to treat digestive issues and other ailments.

Benefits:

Grapes and wine are rich in antioxidants, particularly resveratrol, which has been shown to promote heart health and reduce inflammation. Moderate consumption of wine has been linked to improved digestive health and a reduced risk of certain diseases. However, it is important to note that excessive consumption can have adverse health effects.

Pomegranates

Pomegranates are mentioned in the Bible as symbols of fertility and abundance, and their health benefits were well recognized. In Song of Solomon 4:3, the beauty and health of the bride are compared to a pomegranate: "Thy lips are like a thread of scarlet, and thy speech is comely: thy temples are like a piece of a pomegranate within thy locks."

Historical Context and Uses:

Pomegranates were prized in the ancient world for their juicy seeds and vibrant color. They were consumed fresh, as juice, or dried. The seeds and juice were also used in various medicinal preparations to treat ailments such as digestive disorders and infections.

Benefits:

Pomegranates are rich in vitamins, minerals, and antioxidants, particularly punicalagins and anthocyanins. These compounds have powerful anti-inflammatory and anticancer properties. Pomegranate juice has been shown to improve heart health, reduce blood pressure, and enhance immune function.

Herbs and Spices

Various herbs and spices mentioned in the Old Testament were used for their medicinal properties. These include hyssop, cumin, and coriander.

Hyssop:

In Psalm 51:7, hyssop is associated with purification: "Purge me with hyssop, and I shall be clean: wash me, and I shall be whiter than snow." Hyssop was used in religious rituals and as a medicinal herb for respiratory and digestive ailments.

Cumin and Coriander:

Cumin and coriander were used as spices and for their health benefits. Isaiah 28:25,27 mentions cumin and other herbs: "When he hath made plain the face thereof, doth he not cast abroad the fitches, and scatter the cummin, and cast in the principal wheat and the appointed barley and the rie in their place? For the fitches are not threshed with a threshing instrument, neither is a cart wheel turned about upon the cummin; but the fitches are beaten out with a staff, and the cummin with a rod."

Benefits:

Herbs and spices like hyssop, cumin, and coriander contain essential oils and bioactive compounds that have antimicrobial, anti-inflammatory, and antioxidant properties.

They have been used traditionally to treat digestive issues, and respiratory conditions, and to enhance overall health.

The Old Testament provides numerous examples of foods that were valued not only for their nutritional content but also for their healing properties. Honey, olive oil, figs, grapes, pomegranates, and various herbs and spices were integral to the diet and medicinal practices of ancient Israel. These foods, revered for their divine provision and health benefits, offer a glimpse into the holistic approach to health and healing in biblical times. By understanding the historical and medicinal context of these healing foods, we can appreciate their enduring significance and explore ways to incorporate their benefits into our modern lives.

The Old Testament is rich with narratives that highlight the healing properties of various foods. These stories not only demonstrate the practical use of food for health and healing but also underscore the divine provision and wisdom embedded in the dietary practices of ancient Israel. This chapter explores specific biblical stories and references that showcase the healing power of these foods.

Honey

Honey is prominently featured in the Bible as a symbol of abundance and healing. One of the most illustrative stories involving honey is found in 1 Samuel 14. During a battle against the Philistines, Jonathan, the son of King Saul, unknowingly violates his father's command to abstain from food. Famished, Jonathan finds honey in the forest and eats it, immediately regaining his strength.

1 Samuel 14:27: "But Jonathan had not heard that his father had bound the people with the oath. So he reached out the end of the staff that was in his hand and dipped it into the honeycomb. He raised his hand to his mouth, and his eyes brightened."

This passage illustrates the immediate revitalizing effect of honey, highlighting its role as a natural energy booster and restorative food. The phrase "his eyes brightened" signifies the quick restoration of Jonathan's vigor and alertness, emphasizing honey's nourishing and revitalizing properties.

Olive Oil

Olive oil is frequently mentioned in the Bible for its anointing and healing properties. One notable instance is found in the story of the Good Samaritan in the New Testament, which draws on Old Testament practices. In this parable, Jesus describes how a Samaritan uses oil to treat the wounds of a man who had been beaten and left for dead.

Luke 10:34: "He went to him and bandaged his wounds, pouring on oil and wine. Then he put the man on his own donkey, brought him to an inn and took care of him."

This parable not only highlights the compassionate use of olive oil for healing wounds but also reflects the broader biblical tradition of using oil for medicinal purposes. Olive oil's anti-inflammatory and antimicrobial properties make it an ideal remedy for treating injuries and promoting healing.

Figs

The story of King Hezekiah's illness and recovery provides a compelling example of the medicinal use of figs. When Hezekiah falls ill, the prophet Isaiah prescribes a poultice of figs to heal him.

2 Kings 20:7: "Then Isaiah said, 'Prepare a poultice of figs.' They did so and applied it to the boil, and he recovered."

This narrative underscores the practical application of figs in ancient medicine. The fig poultice likely used for its soothing and anti-inflammatory properties, effectively treats Hezekiah's condition. This story not only highlights the medicinal use of figs but also reinforces the belief in God's guidance in providing natural remedies for healing.

Grapes and Wine

Grapes and wine are frequently mentioned in the Bible, both as symbols of joy and as practical remedies for various ailments. One of the most explicit references to the medicinal use of wine is found in Paul's advice to Timothy.

1 Timothy 5:23: "Stop drinking only water, and use a little wine because of your stomach and your frequent illnesses."

This verse illustrates the recognition of wine's therapeutic properties in the ancient world. Wine, known for its antiseptic and digestive benefits, was recommended to aid digestion and alleviate stomach issues. Paul's advice reflects a common understanding of wine's role in promoting health and well-being.

Pomegranates

Pomegranates are mentioned several times in the Bible, often symbolizing fertility and abundance. While there are no explicit stories detailing their medicinal use, their inclusion in the diet and their symbolic significance suggest an appreciation of their health benefits. The Song of Solomon poetically references the beauty and health associated with pomegranates.

Song of Solomon 4:3: "Your lips are like a scarlet ribbon; your mouth is lovely. Your temples behind your veil are like the halves of a pomegranate."

This poetic imagery associates pomegranates with beauty and vitality, hinting at their nourishing and health-promoting qualities. Pomegranates, rich in vitamins and antioxidants, were likely valued for their ability to enhance health and well-being.

Herbs and Spices

Various herbs and spices mentioned in the Old Testament were used for their healing properties. One significant herb is hyssop, associated with purification and healing.

Psalm 51:7: "Cleanse me with hyssop, and I will be clean; wash me, and I will be whiter than snow."

Hyssop was used in religious rituals for purification, as well as in medicinal preparations for its antiseptic and anti-inflammatory properties. The use of hyssop in this verse symbolizes spiritual cleansing and physical healing, reflecting its dual role in biblical tradition.

The Old Testament provides numerous examples of foods that were considered not only nourishing but also healing. Honey, olive oil, figs, grapes, pomegranates, and various herbs and spices were integral to the diet and medicinal practices of ancient Israel. These foods, revered for their divine provision and health benefits, offer a glimpse into the holistic approach to health and healing in biblical times.

By understanding the historical and medicinal context of these healing foods, we can appreciate their enduring significance and explore ways to incorporate their benefits into our modern lives. The stories and references showcasing the healing power of these foods serve as a testament to the wisdom embedded in biblical dietary practices and the importance of divine provision in promoting health and well-being.

CHAPTER 03

HEALING FOODS IN THE NEW TESTAMENT

The New Testament continues the rich tradition of using food for nourishment and healing, with particular emphasis on the ministry of Jesus Christ. Throughout His ministry, Jesus utilized food in various miraculous healings and teachings, demonstrating the profound significance of food in both physical and spiritual contexts. This chapter explores specific foods associated with Jesus' ministry and healing miracles, illustrating how these foods contributed to His message of compassion, provision, and divine power.

Bread and Fish

Bread and fish are prominently featured in the New Testament, particularly in the context of Jesus' miraculous feedings of the multitudes. These miracles not only addressed the immediate physical hunger of the people but also symbolized the spiritual sustenance that Jesus offers.

Feeding the Five Thousand:

One of the most well-known miracles is the feeding of the five thousand, recorded in all four Gospels. In this event, Jesus takes five loaves of bread and two fish, blesses them, and distributes them to a large crowd. Remarkably, everyone eats their fill, and twelve baskets of leftovers are collected.

Matthew 14:19-20: "And he directed the people to sit down on the grass. Taking the five loaves and the two fish and looking up to heaven, he gave thanks and broke the loaves. Then he gave them to the disciples, and the disciples gave them to the people. They all ate and were satisfied, and the disciples picked up twelve basketfuls of broken pieces that were left over."

This miracle underscores Jesus' ability to provide abundantly for physical needs while also pointing to His role as the Bread of Life, offering eternal sustenance. The bread and fish, staples of the diet in Galilee, become symbols of Jesus' miraculous provision and His concern for both the physical and spiritual well-being of the people.

Feeding the Four Thousand:

A similar miracle occurs in the feeding of the four thousand, where Jesus multiplies seven loaves of bread and a few small fish to feed another large crowd.

Mark 8:6-8: "He told the crowd to sit down on the ground. When he had taken the seven loaves and given thanks, he broke them and gave them to his disciples to distribute to the people, and they did so. They had a few small fish as well; he gave thanks for them also and told the disciples to distribute them. The people ate and were satisfied. Afterward, the disciples picked up seven basketfuls of broken pieces that were left over."

These miracles emphasize the recurring theme of Jesus as the provider and healer, meeting the physical hunger of the people while also addressing their deeper spiritual needs.

Wine

Wine is another significant food in the New Testament, symbolizing joy, blessing, and healing. One of the most notable instances of Jesus using wine is at the wedding in Cana, where He performs His first recorded miracle by turning water into wine.

John 2:9-10: "The master of the banquet tasted the water that had been turned into wine. He did not realize where it had come from, though the servants who had drawn the water knew. Then he called the bridegroom aside and said, 'Everyone brings out the choice wine first and then the cheaper wine after the guests have had too much to drink; but you have saved the best till now.'"

This miracle not only demonstrates Jesus' divine power but also symbolizes the new covenant He brings, one characterized by abundant life and joy. Wine, a common element in Jewish celebrations and rituals, becomes a symbol of the transformative power of Jesus' ministry.

Wine is also central to the Last Supper, where Jesus uses it to symbolize His bloodshed for the salvation of humanity.

Matthew 26:27-28: "Then he took a cup, and when he had given thanks, he gave it to them, saying, 'Drink from it, all of you. This is my blood of the covenant, which is poured out for many for the forgiveness of sins.'"

In this context, wine signifies not only physical nourishment but also spiritual redemption and the promise of eternal life.

Bread

Bread, a staple food in the ancient Near East, carries deep symbolic meaning in the New Testament. Jesus often used bread in His teachings and miracles, illustrating profound spiritual truths through this common food.

The Bread of Life Discourse:

In John 6, following the feeding of the five thousand, Jesus delivers the Bread of Life discourse, where He declares Himself as the true bread from heaven.

John 6:35: "Then Jesus declared, 'I am the bread of life. Whoever comes to me will never go hungry, and whoever believes in me will never be thirsty.'"

This declaration links the physical nourishment provided by bread to the spiritual sustenance that Jesus offers. He presents Himself as the essential source of life and satisfaction, far surpassing the temporary fulfillment of physical hunger.

The Last Supper:

During the Last Supper, Jesus breaks bread and shares it with His disciples, instituting the Eucharist or Holy Communion.

Luke 22:19: "And he took bread, gave thanks and broke it, and gave it to them, saying, 'This is my body given for you; do this in remembrance of me.'"

In this act, bread becomes a powerful symbol of Jesus' sacrificial love and His presence among His followers. The breaking of bread signifies the breaking of His body on the cross, offering salvation and eternal life to all who believe.

Fish

Fish, often paired with bread, also plays a significant role in Jesus' ministry. Beyond the feeding miracles, fish is featured in several post-resurrection appearances of Jesus, reinforcing its symbolic and practical importance.

Post-Resurrection Appearance:

After His resurrection, Jesus appears to His disciples by the Sea of Galilee, where He facilitates a miraculous catch of fish and prepares a meal for them.

John 21:9-13: "When they landed, they saw a fire of burning coals there with fish on it, and some bread. Jesus said to them, 'Bring some of the fish you have just caught.' So Simon Peter climbed back into the boat and dragged the net ashore. It was full of large fish, 153, but even with so many the net was not torn. Jesus said to them, 'Come and have breakfast.' None of the disciples dared ask him, 'Who are you?' They knew it was the Lord. Jesus came, took the bread and gave it to them, and did the same with the fish."

This event emphasizes Jesus' ongoing provision and care for His disciples. The shared meal reinforces their fellowship and mission, illustrating how Jesus continues to nourish and support His followers even after His resurrection.

Healing Miracles Involving Food

While many of Jesus' miracles involved healing through touch or word, some also incorporated food, highlighting the integral role of nourishment in physical and spiritual health.

Healing the Blind Man:

In one instance, Jesus uses a combination of saliva and mud to heal a blind man.

John 9:6-7: "After saying this, he spit on the ground, made some mud with the saliva, and put it on the man's eyes. 'Go,' he told him, 'wash in the Pool of Siloam' (this word means 'Sent'). So the man went and washed, and came home seeing."

While not food in the conventional sense, this miracle demonstrates Jesus' creative use of natural elements to bring about healing, reflecting the broader biblical theme of God's provision through creation.

The New Testament richly illustrates the healing and nourishing power of food through the ministry of Jesus. Bread and fish, wine, and other elements play significant roles in His miracles and teachings, symbolizing both physical sustenance and spiritual nourishment. Through these foods, Jesus not only addresses the immediate needs of the people but also conveys deeper truths about His identity and mission. By understanding these biblical stories and references, we can appreciate the profound significance of food in the New

Testament and its enduring relevance to our faith and daily lives.

Apostolic Teachings on Food and Health in the Early Church

The New Testament not only recounts the ministry of Jesus and His use of food in miraculous healings but also provides insights into the teachings of the apostles regarding food and health in the early Christian community. These teachings highlight the continuation of biblical dietary principles, the role of food in fellowship and worship, and the evolving understanding of dietary laws in light of the new covenant established by Jesus.

The Jerusalem Council and Dietary Laws

One of the most significant events concerning dietary practices in the early church is the Jerusalem Council, recorded in Acts 15. As Gentiles began to convert to Christianity, questions arose about whether they needed to adhere to Jewish dietary laws. The apostles and elders gathered to address this issue, resulting in a pivotal decision for the early church.

Acts 15:28-29: "It seemed good to the Holy Spirit and to us not to burden you with anything beyond the following requirements: You are to abstain from food sacrificed to idols, from blood, from the meat of strangled animals, and from sexual immorality. You will do well to avoid these things."

This decision reflects a balance between respect for Jewish traditions and the freedom of Gentile converts. By focusing on key prohibitions rather than the entire body of kosher laws, the early church established guidelines that promoted health, purity, and unity without imposing the full weight of Jewish dietary restrictions on Gentile believers.

Paul's Teachings on Food and Liberty

The apostle Paul addressed dietary issues extensively in his letters, emphasizing Christian liberty while also advocating for sensitivity and love within the community. His teachings provide valuable insights into the early church's approach to food and health.

Liberty and Sensitivity:

In Romans 14, Paul discusses the differing views on food among believers and urges them to respect each other's consciences.

Romans 14:14-15: "I am convinced, being fully persuaded in the Lord Jesus, that nothing is unclean in itself. But if anyone regards something as unclean, then for that person it is unclean. If your brother or sister is distressed because of what you eat, you are no longer acting in love. Do not by your eating destroy someone for whom Christ died."

Paul's message emphasizes the importance of love and unity over personal freedom. While believers are free to eat all foods, they should be mindful of the impact on others, especially those with sensitive consciences. This teaching underscores the relational and communal aspects of food in the early church.

Food Sacrificed to Idols:

Another major issue Paul addresses is the consumption of food sacrificed to idols. In 1 Corinthians 8, he acknowledges that while idols are not real gods, and therefore food sacrificed to them is not inherently tainted, the practice could be a stumbling block for weaker believers.

1 Corinthians 8:9-13: "Be careful, however, that the exercise of your rights does not become a stumbling block to the weak. For if someone with a weak conscience sees you, with all your knowledge, eating in an idol's temple, won't that person be emboldened to eat what is sacrificed to idols? So this weak brother or sister, for whom Christ died, is destroyed by your knowledge. When you sin against them in this way and wound their weak conscience, you sin against Christ. Therefore, if what I eat causes my brother or sister to fall into sin, I will never eat meat again, so that I will not cause them to fall."

Paul's guidance here is practical and pastoral, highlighting the need for sensitivity and the prioritization of others' spiritual well-being over personal dietary practices.

Communal Meals and Fellowship

Communal meals, or agape feasts, were central to the life of the early church. These gatherings were not only opportunities for fellowship and mutual support but also occasions for worship and remembrance of Jesus' sacrifice.

Acts 2:46-47: "Every day they continued to meet together in the temple courts. They broke bread in their homes and ate together with glad and sincere hearts, praising God and enjoying the favor of all the people. And the Lord added to their number daily those who were being saved."

These meals fostered a sense of community and equality, as believers shared their resources and supported one another. The breaking of bread, a practice initiated by Jesus at the Last Supper, was central to these gatherings, symbolizing their unity in Christ and their shared hope in His return.

The Lord's Supper

The Lord's Supper, or Eucharist, was a foundational practice in the early church, instituted by Jesus as a means of remembering His sacrifice and celebrating the new covenant. Paul provides instructions for this practice in 1 Corinthians

11, emphasizing its significance and the proper attitude with which it should be observed.

1 Corinthians 11:23-26: "For I received from the Lord what I also passed on to you: The Lord Jesus, on the night he was betrayed, took bread, and when he had given thanks, he broke it and said, 'This is my body, which is for you; do this in remembrance of me.' In the same way, after supper he took the cup, saying, 'This cup is the new covenant in my blood; do this, whenever you drink it, in remembrance of me.' For whenever you eat this bread and drink this cup, you proclaim the Lord's death until he comes."

Paul's instructions highlight the Lord's Supper as a time of reflection, gratitude, and proclamation of the gospel. This practice reinforced the centrality of Jesus' sacrifice and the communal nature of the Christian faith.

Health and Holiness

The apostles also taught that the body is a temple of the Holy Spirit, emphasizing the importance of health and holiness. Paul's teachings encourage believers to honor God with their bodies, which includes mindful eating and overall health.

1 Corinthians 6:19-20: "Do you not know that your bodies are temples of the Holy Spirit, who is in you, whom

you have received from God? You are not your own; you were bought at a price. Therefore honor God with your bodies."

This perspective fosters an understanding of health and well-being as integral to spiritual life. Maintaining physical health through proper nutrition and care for the body is seen as a way to honor God and enhance one's ability to serve Him and the community.

The apostolic teachings on food and health in the early church reflect a deep understanding of the interconnectedness of physical and spiritual well-being. By navigating issues of dietary laws, communal meals, and the significance of the Lord's Supper, the apostles provided a framework for the early Christians to live in harmony, health, and holiness. These teachings continue to offer valuable insights for modern believers, emphasizing the importance of food in fostering community, honoring God, and promoting holistic health. By integrating these principles into our lives, we can better appreciate the enduring wisdom of the early church and its relevance to our contemporary context.

CHAPTER 04

HERBS AND PLANTS IN BIBLICAL HEALING

The Bible mentions numerous herbs and plants that were used for their medicinal properties in ancient times. These natural remedies were integral to the health practices of the people in biblical times and provided valuable insights into the holistic approach to healing that characterized biblical medicine. This chapter explores the detailed uses of various herbs and plants mentioned in the Bible, highlighting their historical context, medicinal properties, and their relevance to modern herbal medicine.

Hyssop

Hyssop is one of the most frequently mentioned herbs in the Bible, known for its cleansing and purifying properties. It appears in both ritualistic and medicinal contexts.

Historical Context and Uses:

Hyssop was used in purification rituals, particularly in the cleansing of lepers and the purification of houses infected with mildew. In the Passover story, hyssop was used to apply the blood of the sacrificial lamb to the doorposts, symbolizing protection and purification.

Exodus 12:22: "Take a bunch of hyssop, dip it into the blood in the basin, and put some of the blood on the top and on both sides of the doorframe."

Psalm 51:7: "Cleanse me with hyssop, and I will be clean; wash me, and I will be whiter than snow."

Medicinal Properties:

Hyssop has antiseptic, anti-inflammatory, and expectorant properties. It was used to treat respiratory conditions, such as bronchitis and asthma, and to aid in digestion. Modern herbal medicine recognizes hyssop as a beneficial herb for its ability to soothe sore throats, alleviate coughs, and support the respiratory system.

Myrrh

Myrrh is another significant plant in the Bible, noted for its aromatic and medicinal qualities. It was one of the gifts brought by the wise men to the infant Jesus, symbolizing its value and importance.

Historical Context and Uses:

Myrrh was used in anointing oils, perfumes, and embalming practices. It was a key ingredient in the holy anointing oil described in Exodus.

Exodus 30:23-25: "Take the following fine spices: 500 shekels of liquid myrrh, half as much (that is, 250 shekels) of fragrant cinnamon, 250 shekels of fragrant calamus, 500 shekels of cassia—all according to the sanctuary shekel—and a hin of olive oil. Make these into a sacred anointing oil, a fragrant blend, the work of a perfumer. It will be the sacred anointing oil."

Medicinal Properties:

Myrrh has strong antiseptic and anti-inflammatory properties. It was traditionally used to treat wounds, infections, and digestive issues. Modern studies have confirmed myrrh's effectiveness in wound healing, reducing inflammation, and alleviating pain.

Frankincense

Frankincense, like myrrh, is an aromatic resin mentioned in the Bible for its use in incense, perfumes, and medicinal preparations. It was another gift from the wise men to Jesus.

Historical Context and Uses:

Frankincense was burned as incense in religious ceremonies and used in sacred rituals. It was also valued for its healing properties.

Matthew 2:11: "On coming to the house, they saw the child with his mother Mary, and they bowed down and worshiped him. Then they opened their treasures and presented him with gifts of gold, frankincense and myrrh."

Medicinal Properties:

Frankincense has anti-inflammatory, antiseptic, and analgesic properties. It was used to treat respiratory conditions, skin disorders, and digestive issues. In modern herbal medicine, frankincense is used to support the immune system, reduce inflammation, and improve respiratory health.

Aloe

Aloe is mentioned in the Bible for its fragrant and medicinal qualities. It was used in burial practices and for its healing properties.

Historical Context and Uses:

Aloe was used in combination with myrrh for embalming purposes, as seen in the burial of Jesus.

John 19:39: "He was accompanied by Nicodemus, the man who earlier had visited Jesus at night. Nicodemus brought a mixture of myrrh and aloes, about seventy-five pounds."

Medicinal Properties:

Aloe is well-known for its soothing and healing properties, particularly for skin conditions. It is used to treat burns, wounds, and skin irritations. Aloe also has anti-inflammatory and antibacterial properties, making it a valuable plant in both ancient and modern medicine.

Mint, Dill, and Cumin

These herbs are mentioned in the context of tithing and culinary use, but they also have medicinal applications.

Historical Context and Uses:

Mint, dill, and cumin were commonly used as flavoring agents and for their healing properties. Jesus mentions them in His critique of the Pharisees' emphasis on minor laws over justice and mercy.

Matthew 23:23: "Woe to you, teachers of the law and Pharisees, you hypocrites! You give a tenth of your spices—mint, dill, and cumin. But you have neglected the more important matters of the law—justice, mercy, and faithfulness. You should have practiced the latter, without neglecting the former."

Medicinal Properties:

- Mint: Known for its soothing effects on the digestive system, mint was used to relieve indigestion, nausea, and headaches.

- Dill: Dill has antibacterial properties and was used to soothe digestive issues and treat colic in infants.

- Cumin: Cumin is rich in antioxidants and has anti-inflammatory properties. It was used to aid digestion, boost the immune system, and treat various ailments.

Balm of Gilead

The Balm of Gilead is a legendary medicinal compound mentioned in the Bible, renowned for its healing properties.

Historical Context and Uses:

The balm was derived from the resin of certain trees and was highly valued for its soothing and healing qualities.

Jeremiah 8:22: "Is there no balm in Gilead? Is there no physician there? Why then is there no healing for the wound of my people?"

Medicinal Properties:

The Balm of Gilead was used to treat wounds, infections, and inflammation. It was known for its soothing properties and was often applied to cuts, bruises, and other skin ailments.

The herbs and plants mentioned in the Bible for their medicinal purposes reflect a deep understanding of the healing properties of natural remedies. Hyssop, myrrh, frankincense, aloe, mint, dill, cumin, and the Balm of Gilead are just a few examples of the rich botanical knowledge embedded in biblical texts. These plants were used not only for their physical healing properties but also in religious rituals and daily practices, highlighting the holistic approach to health and well-being in biblical times. By exploring these ancient remedies, we can appreciate the enduring wisdom of biblical healing and find inspiration for incorporating these natural solutions into our modern lives.

Their Historical and Cultural Significance

The Bible contains numerous references to herbs and plants, underscoring their essential role in the daily lives, health practices, and spiritual rituals of ancient peoples. These natural resources were not only valued for their medicinal properties but also held deep cultural and symbolic significance. This chapter delves into the historical and cultural importance of various herbs and plants mentioned in the Bible, highlighting how they were used and revered in biblical times.

Hyssop

Hyssop is a plant frequently mentioned in the Bible, often associated with purification and cleansing. Its significance extends beyond its medicinal properties, embedding itself deeply into the religious and cultural practices of the Israelites.

Historical and Cultural Significance:

Hyssop's primary use in biblical times was in purification rites. It was used to sprinkle blood during Passover and in the cleansing of lepers and houses infected with mildew.

Exodus 12:22: "Take a bunch of hyssop, dip it into the blood in the basin and put some of the blood on the top and on both sides of the doorframe."

Leviticus 14:4: "Then the priest shall command to take for him that is to be cleansed two birds alive and clean, and cedar wood, and scarlet, and hyssop."

In these contexts, hyssop symbolizes spiritual cleansing and renewal, reinforcing its importance in the religious life of the community. Its use in these rites highlights a cultural understanding of purity that intertwines physical and spiritual health.

Myrrh

Myrrh, a resin obtained from certain trees, is mentioned numerous times in the Bible. It was highly valued for its aromatic qualities and medicinal properties, making it a significant commodity in the ancient world.

Historical and Cultural Significance:

Myrrh was used in a variety of ways, from religious rituals to medicinal applications. It was a key ingredient in the holy anointing oil described in Exodus and was also used in embalming practices, most notably in the burial of Jesus.

Matthew 2:11: "On coming to the house, they saw the child with his mother Mary, and they bowed down and worshiped him. Then they opened their treasures and presented him with gifts of gold, frankincense and myrrh."

John 19:39: "He was accompanied by Nicodemus, the man who earlier had visited Jesus at night. Nicodemus brought a mixture of myrrh and aloes, about seventy-five pounds."

Myrrh's use in anointing and embalming highlights its role in the sacred and the profane, bridging the gap between life and death. Its aromatic and preservative properties made it essential in burial rites, symbolizing purification and honoring the deceased.

Frankincense

Frankincense, like myrrh, is a resin that was highly prized in the ancient world. Its primary use was in incense, but it also had significant medicinal applications.

Historical and Cultural Significance:

Frankincense was a major component of the incense used in temple worship, signifying prayers ascending to heaven.

Exodus 30:34-36: "Then the Lord said to Moses, 'Take fragrant spices—gum resin, onycha and galbanum—and pure frankincense, all in equal amounts, and make a fragrant blend of incense, the work of a perfumer. It is to be salted and pure and sacred.'"

The use of frankincense in worship underscores its symbolic role as a connector between the human and the divine. It was also used medicinally to treat a variety of ailments, reinforcing its importance in both health and spirituality.

Aloe

Aloe, mentioned in the context of burial practices, was valued for its fragrant and healing properties.

Historical and Cultural Significance:

Aloe was used in the embalming process, indicating its significance in preserving and honoring the dead.

John 19:39-40: "Nicodemus brought a mixture of myrrh and aloes, about seventy-five pounds. Taking Jesus' body, the two of them wrapped it, with the spices, in strips of linen. This was in accordance with Jewish burial customs."

Aloe's use of embalming reflects a cultural emphasis on respect for the dead and the belief in an afterlife, where the preservation of the body was seen as an important aspect of the burial ritual.

Mint, Dill, and Cumin

These herbs, commonly used in culinary and medicinal contexts, were also mentioned in the context of tithing, reflecting their economic and cultural value.

Historical and Cultural Significance:

Mint, dill, and cumin were staples in the diet and medicine of the ancient Near East. Their mention in the context of tithing by Jesus underscores their everyday significance.

Matthew 23:23: "Woe to you, teachers of the law and Pharisees, you hypocrites! You give a tenth of your spices—mint, dill and cumin. But you have neglected the more important matters of the law—justice, mercy and faithfulness. You should have practiced the latter, without neglecting the former."

These herbs were important not only for their flavor and medicinal properties but also as valuable commodities. Their use in tithing reflects their integral role in daily life and their economic importance.

Balm of Gilead

The Balm of Gilead, a resinous substance, was renowned for its healing properties and is mentioned in the Bible as a symbol of healing and comfort.

Historical and Cultural Significance:

The balm was produced in the region of Gilead and was highly sought after for its soothing and healing properties.

Jeremiah 8:22: "Is there no balm in Gilead? Is there no physician there? Why then is there no healing for the wound of my people?"

The Balm of Gilead symbolizes hope and healing, often used metaphorically to represent God's provision of comfort and restoration. Its high value and sought-after status highlight its importance in ancient medical practices.

Mustard Seed

The mustard seed, though a small and seemingly insignificant herb, carries significant symbolic weight in the teachings of Jesus.

Historical and Cultural Significance:

Jesus used the mustard seed to illustrate the power of faith, emphasizing that even the smallest amount of faith can achieve great things.

Matthew 17:20: "He replied, 'Because you have so little faith. Truly I tell you, if you have faith as small as a mustard seed, you can say to this mountain, 'Move from here to there,' and it will move. Nothing will be impossible for you.'"

The mustard seed's cultural significance lies in its representation of growth and potential. Despite its small size, it grows into a large plant, symbolizing the expansive and transformative power of faith.

The herbs and plants mentioned in the Bible hold profound historical and cultural significance. Hyssop, myrrh, frankincense, aloe, mint, dill, cumin, the Balm of Gilead, and mustard seed were integral to the health practices, religious rituals, and daily lives of the people in biblical times. These natural remedies were not only valued for their physical healing properties but also imbued with symbolic meanings that reinforced the spiritual and cultural beliefs of the community. By understanding the historical and cultural contexts of these herbs and plants, we can appreciate the holistic approach to health and healing that characterized biblical medicine and find inspiration for incorporating these ancient practices into our modern lives.

CHAPTER 05

DIETARY WISDOM AND HEALTH BENEFITS

The Bible offers a rich tapestry of dietary principles that not only provided nourishment to ancient communities but also promoted health and well-being. These principles, rooted in divine wisdom, have been validated by modern nutritional science, highlighting their timeless relevance. This chapter analyzes the nutritional and health benefits of biblical dietary principles, illustrating how these ancient guidelines can contribute to a healthy and balanced lifestyle.

Clean and Unclean Foods

One of the foundational aspects of biblical dietary wisdom is the distinction between clean and unclean foods, as outlined in Leviticus 11 and Deuteronomy 14. These laws were not arbitrary but based on practical health considerations.

Nutritional and Health Benefits:

- Clean Animals: Animals considered clean, such as cattle, sheep, and goats, are herbivores that typically have lower levels of toxins in their flesh compared to omnivores or carnivores. These animals often graze on grasses and plants, resulting in leaner meat with beneficial nutrients like omega-3 fatty acids.

- Unclean Animals: Animals deemed unclean, such as pigs and shellfish, can carry higher risks of diseases and parasites. Pigs, for instance, are prone to trichinosis, a parasitic disease that can be transmitted to humans through undercooked pork. Shellfish can accumulate toxins from their environment, posing risks of foodborne illnesses.

By avoiding unclean animals, the Israelites minimized the risk of consuming harmful pathogens and toxins, promoting overall health and reducing the incidence of foodborne diseases.

Emphasis on Plant-Based Foods

The biblical diet places a strong emphasis on plant-based foods, including grains, fruits, vegetables, nuts, and seeds. This emphasis aligns with modern dietary recommendations that highlight the benefits of plant-based nutrition.

Genesis 1:29: "Then God said, 'I give you every seed-bearing plant on the face of the whole earth and every tree that has fruit with seed in it. They will be yours for food.'"

Nutritional and Health Benefits:

- Grains and Legumes: Whole grains like barley and wheat, along with legumes such as lentils and beans, are rich in fiber, vitamins, and minerals. They provide sustained energy, promote digestive health, and help regulate blood sugar levels.

- Fruits and Vegetables: Fruits and vegetables are packed with essential nutrients, antioxidants, and phytochemicals that support immune function, reduce inflammation, and protect against chronic diseases.

- Nuts and Seeds: Nuts and seeds, such as almonds and flaxseeds, are excellent sources of healthy fats, protein, and essential micronutrients. They support heart health, brain function, and overall well-being.

By prioritizing plant-based foods, the biblical diet promotes a nutrient-dense, balanced approach to eating that supports long-term health.

Moderation and Balanced Consumption

The Bible advocates for moderation and balance in food consumption, warning against gluttony and excessive indulgence. Proverbs, in particular, emphasizes the importance of self-control and wise eating habits.

Proverbs 23:20-21: "Do not join those who drink too much wine or gorge themselves on meat, for drunkards and gluttons become poor, and drowsiness clothes them in rags."

Nutritional and Health Benefits:

- Weight Management: Practicing moderation helps maintain a healthy weight, reducing the risk of obesity and related health conditions such as heart disease, diabetes, and hypertension.

- Digestive Health: Balanced consumption prevents overloading the digestive system, promoting efficient digestion and nutrient absorption.

- Mental Well-being: Moderation fosters a healthy relationship with food, reducing stress and anxiety related to eating habits.

By advocating for moderation, the Bible encourages mindful eating practices that contribute to overall health and well-being.

Use of Natural and Whole Foods

The biblical diet emphasizes the use of natural and whole foods, minimally processed and free from artificial additives. This principle aligns with contemporary dietary advice that encourages the consumption of whole, unprocessed foods for optimal health.

Nutritional and Health Benefits:

- Nutrient Density: Whole foods retain their natural nutrient content, providing essential vitamins, minerals, and antioxidants that support various bodily functions.

- Reduced Additives: Minimally processed foods are free from artificial additives, preservatives, and unhealthy fats that can negatively impact health.

- Improved Digestive Health: Whole foods, rich in fiber, promote digestive health and prevent issues such as constipation and bloating.

By focusing on natural and whole foods, the biblical diet supports a clean, nutrient-rich approach to eating that fosters long-term health.

Regular Fasting and Its Benefits

Fasting is a practice mentioned in the Bible that has both spiritual and physical benefits. Regular periods of fasting were observed for spiritual reflection, repentance, and seeking God's guidance.

Isaiah 58:6: "Is not this the kind of fasting I have chosen: to loose the chains of injustice and untie the cords of the yoke, to set the oppressed free and break every yoke?"

Nutritional and Health Benefits:

- Detoxification: Fasting allows the body to detoxify, clearing out toxins and supporting liver function.

- Metabolic Health: Intermittent fasting has been shown to improve insulin sensitivity, support weight management, and reduce the risk of metabolic diseases.

- Cellular Repair: Fasting promotes autophagy, a process where cells remove damaged components, enhancing cellular repair and longevity.

The practice of fasting, as advocated in the Bible, offers significant health benefits, supporting both physical and spiritual well-being.

Specific Healing Foods

The Bible mentions specific foods that were recognized for their healing properties, many of which are supported by modern scientific research.

Honey:

Honey is frequently mentioned for its sweetness and healing qualities.

Proverbs 24:13: "Eat honey, my son, for it is good; honey from the comb is sweet to your taste."

Health Benefits:

Honey has antibacterial, anti-inflammatory, and antioxidant properties. It can soothe sore throats, heal wounds, and provide a natural energy boost.

Olive Oil:

Olive oil is used for anointing and medicinal purposes.

Ezekiel 16:13: "So you were adorned with gold and silver; your clothes were of fine linen and costly fabric and embroidered cloth. Your food was fine flour, honey, and olive oil."

Health Benefits:

Olive oil is rich in monounsaturated fats and antioxidants. It supports heart health, reduces inflammation, and promotes overall well-being.

Garlic:

While not explicitly mentioned in the Bible, garlic was a staple in ancient diets and is known for its medicinal properties.

Health Benefits:

Garlic has antimicrobial, antiviral, and anti-inflammatory properties. It supports cardiovascular health, boosts the immune system, and has been shown to reduce the risk of certain cancers.

The dietary principles found in the Bible offer a holistic approach to nutrition and health, emphasizing clean and unclean foods, plant-based diets, moderation, natural and whole foods, and the benefits of fasting. These guidelines, rooted in divine wisdom, align closely with modern nutritional science, highlighting their timeless relevance and efficacy. By incorporating these principles into our daily lives, we can promote optimal health, prevent disease, and cultivate a balanced and nourishing approach to eating that honors both our physical and spiritual well-being. The wisdom of biblical dietary practices continues to provide valuable insights for achieving a healthy and fulfilling life.

Modern Scientific Perspectives on the Healthiness of Biblical Foods

The dietary principles outlined in the Bible have withstood the test of time, and modern scientific research has increasingly validated the health benefits of many foods mentioned in the Scriptures. This chapter explores the healthiness of biblical foods from a contemporary scientific perspective, illustrating how these ancient dietary guidelines align with current nutritional understanding and practices.

Clean and Unclean Foods

The biblical distinction between clean and unclean foods, as found in Leviticus 11 and Deuteronomy 14, aligns with modern food safety and health considerations.

Scientific Validation:

- Clean Animals: The consumption of herbivorous animals such as cattle, sheep, and goats, which are classified as clean in the Bible, is generally considered healthier due to lower fat content and fewer toxins compared to omnivorous or carnivorous animals. These animals tend to have leaner meat rich in protein, essential fatty acids, and nutrients like iron and zinc.

- Unclean Animals: Animals such as pigs and shellfish, deemed unclean in the Bible, are more likely to carry diseases and parasites. Pigs, for instance, can harbor trichinosis, a parasitic disease that can infect humans through undercooked pork. Shellfish can accumulate toxins from their environment, increasing the risk of foodborne illnesses.

Modern food safety guidelines often echo these concerns, recommending proper handling, cooking, and sometimes avoidance of certain high-risk foods to prevent disease.

Emphasis on Plant-Based Foods

The Bible's emphasis on plant-based foods is well supported by modern nutritional science, which advocates for diets rich in fruits, vegetables, whole grains, nuts, and seeds.

Scientific Validation:

- Grains and Legumes: Whole grains such as barley and wheat, along with legumes like lentils and beans, are high in dietary fiber, vitamins, and minerals. They provide long-lasting energy, promote digestive health, and help manage blood sugar levels. The consumption of these foods is linked to reduced risks of heart disease, diabetes, and certain cancers.

- Fruits and Vegetables: Fruits and vegetables are packed with essential nutrients, antioxidants, and phytochemicals that support immune function, reduce inflammation, and protect against chronic diseases. Regular consumption is associated with lower risks of cardiovascular diseases, cancer, and obesity.

- Nuts and Seeds: Nuts and seeds, such as almonds and flaxseeds, are rich in healthy fats, protein, and micronutrients. They support heart health, brain function, and overall well-being. Studies have shown that diets including nuts and seeds can lower cholesterol levels, reduce inflammation, and improve metabolic health.

These plant-based foods form the cornerstone of many modern dietary recommendations, including the Mediterranean diet, which is widely regarded as one of the healthiest eating patterns.

Olive Oil

Olive oil, frequently mentioned in the Bible for its use in cooking, anointing, and medicinal purposes, is a key component of the Mediterranean diet.

Scientific Validation:

Olive oil is rich in monounsaturated fats, particularly oleic acid, which has been shown to reduce inflammation and lower the risk of heart disease. It also contains antioxidants like polyphenols, which protect against oxidative stress and inflammation.

Health Benefits:

- Heart Health: Regular consumption of olive oil is associated with lower levels of bad cholesterol (LDL) and higher levels of good cholesterol (HDL). It also helps reduce blood pressure and improves blood vessel function.

- Anti-Inflammatory Effects: Olive oil's anti-inflammatory properties can help reduce the risk of chronic diseases such as arthritis and Alzheimer's disease.

- Digestive Health: Olive oil promotes healthy digestion and can protect against gastric ulcers and gallstones.

The inclusion of olive oil in the diet is recommended by health organizations for its protective effects against cardiovascular diseases and its overall health benefits.

Honey

Honey, noted in the Bible for its sweetness and medicinal properties, continues to be valued for its health benefits in modern times.

Scientific Validation:

Honey possesses antibacterial, anti-inflammatory, and antioxidant properties. It is used in wound care, cough relief, and as a natural sweetener.

Health Benefits:

- Wound Healing: Honey's antibacterial properties make it effective in promoting wound healing and preventing infections. Manuka honey, in particular, is renowned for its potent healing properties.

- Cough Relief: Honey can soothe sore throats and suppress coughs. It is a common ingredient in natural cough remedies.

- Antioxidant Support: Honey contains antioxidants that help protect the body from oxidative stress, which is linked to aging and the development of diseases like cancer.

The use of honey as a natural remedy aligns with its biblical reputation as a healing food.

Figs

Figs, mentioned in the Bible for their nourishing and healing properties, are rich in dietary fiber, vitamins, and minerals.

Scientific Validation:

Figs are high in fiber, which supports digestive health, and contain essential nutrients such as potassium, calcium, and magnesium.

Health Benefits:

- Digestive Health: The high fiber content in figs helps promote regular bowel movements and prevents constipation. It also supports a healthy gut microbiome.

- Bone Health: Figs provide calcium and magnesium, essential for maintaining strong bones and preventing osteoporosis.

- Blood Pressure Regulation: The potassium in figs helps regulate blood pressure by counteracting the effects of sodium.

Modern nutrition recognizes figs as a beneficial food for maintaining digestive health, supporting bone health, and regulating blood pressure.

Grapes and Wine

Grapes and wine, often mentioned in the Bible, have significant health benefits when consumed in moderation.

Scientific Validation:

Grapes and wine, particularly red wine, contain antioxidants like resveratrol, which have been linked to various health benefits.

Health Benefits:

- Heart Health: Moderate wine consumption is associated with reduced risk of heart disease. The antioxidants in wine help protect the lining of blood vessels and reduce bad cholesterol levels.

- Longevity: Resveratrol has been studied for its potential to extend lifespan and prevent age-related diseases.

- Anti-Inflammatory Effects: The polyphenols in grapes and wine have anti-inflammatory properties that can help reduce the risk of chronic diseases.

While moderation is key, the inclusion of grapes and wine in the diet can contribute to heart health and overall well-being.

Herbs and Spices

Various herbs and spices mentioned in the Bible, such as mint, dill, and cumin, have recognized health benefits.

Scientific Validation:

- Mint: Known for its soothing effects on the digestive system, mint can relieve indigestion, nausea, and headaches.

- Dill: Dill has antibacterial properties and was used to soothe digestive issues and treat colic in infants.

- Cumin: Cumin is rich in antioxidants and has anti-inflammatory properties. It aids digestion, boosts the immune system, and has been shown to reduce the risk of certain diseases.

Health Benefits:

Incorporating herbs and spices into the diet not only enhances flavor but also provides various health benefits, including improved digestion, enhanced immune function, and reduced inflammation.

The dietary wisdom found in the Bible, grounded in divine principles, aligns closely with modern scientific understanding of nutrition and health. Clean and unclean foods, plant-based diets, the use of olive oil, honey, figs, grapes, and herbs, all illustrate the health benefits of these ancient dietary guidelines. By integrating these principles into our modern lifestyles, we can enhance our physical health, prevent disease, and promote overall well-being. The timeless wisdom of biblical dietary practices continues to offer valuable insights for achieving a balanced and healthy life.

CHAPTER 06

RECIPES AND PRACTICAL APPLICATIONS

The dietary wisdom found in the Bible not only offers health benefits but also provides inspiration for delicious and nutritious recipes. This chapter presents a selection of recipes inspired by biblical foods, incorporating the healthful ingredients mentioned in the Scriptures. These recipes are designed to be both tasty and nourishing, helping you integrate the principles of biblical nutrition into your daily meals.

Honey and Olive Oil Bread

Bread is a staple in biblical cuisine, often mentioned in both the Old and New Testaments. This recipe combines the health benefits of honey and olive oil, creating a delicious and wholesome bread.

Ingredients:

- 3 cups whole wheat flour

- 1 cup all-purpose flour

- 2 teaspoons salt

- 2 teaspoons instant yeast

- 1 ½ cups warm water

- ¼ cup honey

- ¼ cup olive oil

Instructions:

1. In a large bowl, mix the whole wheat flour, all-purpose flour, salt, and yeast.

2. In a separate bowl, combine the warm water, honey, and olive oil.

3. Gradually add the wet ingredients to the dry ingredients, mixing until a dough forms.

4. Knead the dough on a floured surface for about 10 minutes, until smooth and elastic.

5. Place the dough in a greased bowl, cover, and let it rise in a warm place for about 1 hour, or until doubled in size.

6. Preheat the oven to 375°F (190°C).

7. Punch down the dough, shape it into a loaf, and place it in a greased loaf pan.

8. Cover and let it rise again for about 30 minutes.

9. Bake for 30-35 minutes, or until the bread sounds hollow when tapped.

10. Let cool before slicing.

Health Benefits:

- Whole Wheat Flour: Rich in fiber, vitamins, and minerals, supporting digestive health and providing sustained energy.

- Honey: Natural sweetener with antibacterial and antioxidant properties.

- Olive Oil: Heart-healthy fats and antioxidants that reduce inflammation.

Lentil and Barley Stew

Lentils and barley are both mentioned in the Bible as nutritious staples. This hearty stew is packed with protein, fiber, and essential nutrients.

Ingredients:

- 1 cup dried lentils, rinsed
- ½ cup pearl barley
- 1 onion, chopped
- 2 cloves garlic, minced
- 2 carrots, chopped
- 2 celery stalks, chopped
- 1 can (14.5 oz) diced tomatoes
- 4 cups vegetable broth
- 1 teaspoon ground cumin
- 1 teaspoon ground coriander
- 1 teaspoon dried thyme

- Salt and pepper to taste

- 2 tablespoons olive oil

- Fresh parsley for garnish

Instructions:

1. In a large pot, heat the olive oil over medium heat. Add the onion, garlic, carrots, and celery, and sauté until softened.

2. Add the lentils, barley, diced tomatoes, vegetable broth, cumin, coriander, thyme, salt, and pepper.

3. Bring to a boil, then reduce heat and simmer for about 45 minutes, or until the lentils and barley are tender.

4. Adjust seasoning as needed.

5. Serve hot, garnished with fresh parsley.

Health Benefits:

- Lentils: High in protein, fiber, and iron, promoting muscle repair and digestive health.

- Barley: Rich in fiber, vitamins, and minerals, supporting heart health and digestion.

- Vegetables: Provide essential vitamins, minerals, and antioxidants.

Fig and Nut Salad

Figs are mentioned in the Bible for their sweetness and nutritional value. This salad combines figs with nuts and leafy greens for a nutrient-packed dish.

Ingredients:

- 6 fresh figs, quartered

- 4 cups mixed leafy greens (spinach, arugula, etc.)

- ½ cup walnuts or almonds, toasted

- ¼ cup crumbled goat cheese (optional)

- 2 tablespoons olive oil

- 1 tablespoon balsamic vinegar

- 1 teaspoon honey

- Salt and pepper to taste

Instructions:

1. In a large bowl, combine the mixed greens, figs, and toasted nuts.

2. In a small bowl, whisk together the olive oil, balsamic vinegar, honey, salt, and pepper.

3. Drizzle the dressing over the salad and toss to combine.

4. Top with crumbled goat cheese, if using.

5. Serve immediately.

Health Benefits:

- Figs: High in fiber, vitamins, and minerals, supporting digestive health and bone strength.

- Nuts: Provide healthy fats, protein, and antioxidants.

- Leafy Greens: Rich in vitamins A, C, and K, promoting overall health.

Grilled Fish with Herbs

Fish is a staple in the New Testament, often associated with Jesus' miracles. This simple recipe uses fresh herbs for flavor and nutrition.

Ingredients:

- 4 fish fillets (such as salmon, trout, or tilapia)

- 2 tablespoons olive oil

- 2 cloves garlic, minced

- 1 tablespoon fresh rosemary, chopped

- 1 tablespoon fresh thyme, chopped

- 1 lemon, sliced

- Salt and pepper to taste

Instructions:

1. Preheat the grill to medium-high heat.

2. In a small bowl, combine the olive oil, garlic, rosemary, thyme, salt, and pepper.

3. Brush the fish fillets with the herb mixture.

4. Place the lemon slices on the grill, then place the fish fillets on top of the lemons.

5. Grill for about 4-5 minutes per side, or until the fish is cooked through and flakes easily with a fork.

6. Serve hot, garnished with additional lemon slices and fresh herbs.

Health Benefits:

- Fish: Rich in omega-3 fatty acids, supporting heart and brain health.

- Herbs: Provide antioxidants and anti-inflammatory properties.

- Olive Oil: Contains healthy fats and antioxidants.

Pomegranate and Quinoa Salad

Pomegranates are praised in the Bible for their health benefits. This vibrant salad combines pomegranate seeds with quinoa and fresh herbs.

Ingredients:

- 1 cup quinoa, rinsed

- 2 cups water

- 1 cup pomegranate seeds

- ½ cup chopped fresh parsley

- ¼ cup chopped fresh mint

- ¼ cup chopped red onion

- 2 tablespoons olive oil

- 1 tablespoon lemon juice

- Salt and pepper to taste

Instructions:

1. In a medium saucepan, bring the quinoa and water to a boil. Reduce heat, cover, and simmer for 15 minutes, or until the quinoa is cooked and water is absorbed. Fluff with a fork and let cool.

2. In a large bowl, combine the cooked quinoa, pomegranate seeds, parsley, mint, and red onion.

3. In a small bowl, whisk together the olive oil, lemon juice, salt, and pepper.

4. Pour the dressing over the salad and toss to combine.

5. Serve chilled or at room temperature.

Health Benefits:

- Quinoa: High in protein, fiber, and essential amino acids, promoting muscle health and digestion.

- Pomegranate: Rich in antioxidants, supporting heart health and reducing inflammation.

- Herbs: Provide vitamins and antioxidants, enhancing overall health.

These recipes, inspired by biblical foods, offer a delicious way to incorporate the health benefits of ancient dietary wisdom into modern meals. By focusing on whole, natural ingredients like honey, olive oil, lentils, barley, figs, fish, and pomegranates, these dishes provide essential nutrients that support overall health and well-being. Embracing these nutritious and flavorful recipes can help you enjoy the benefits of a diet rooted in biblical principles, promoting both physical and spiritual nourishment.

The wisdom found in the Bible regarding food is not just about what to eat, but also how to prepare and consume it. The cooking methods and nutritional insights gleaned from biblical texts align closely with modern health principles. This chapter explores various cooking methods inspired by biblical practices and provides nutritional insights into these methods, along with practical recipes that bring ancient wisdom into contemporary kitchens.

Cooking Methods

1. Grilling and Roasting

2. Stewing and Boiling

3. Baking

4. Fermenting

5. Raw Consumption

Grilling and Roasting

Grilling and roasting are prominent cooking methods in the Bible. These techniques not only enhance the flavor of the food but also retain essential nutrients.

Biblical Example:

In Genesis 18:6-8, Abraham prepares a meal for his divine guests, which likely includes roasted meat.

Nutritional Insights:

- Retains Nutrients: Grilling and roasting at high temperatures help retain water-soluble vitamins (e.g., B vitamins) that can be lost in other cooking methods.

- Enhances Flavor: These methods enhance the natural flavors of the food without needing excessive added fats or oils.

Recipe: Grilled Fish with Herbs

Ingredients:

- 4 fish fillets (such as salmon, trout, or tilapia)

- 2 tablespoons olive oil

- 2 cloves garlic, minced

- 1 tablespoon fresh rosemary, chopped

- 1 tablespoon fresh thyme, chopped

- 1 lemon, sliced

- Salt and pepper to taste

Instructions:

1. Preheat the grill to medium-high heat.

2. In a small bowl, combine the olive oil, garlic, rosemary, thyme, salt, and pepper.

3. Brush the fish fillets with the herb mixture.

4. Place the lemon slices on the grill, then place the fish fillets on top of the lemons.

5. Grill for about 4-5 minutes per side, or until the fish is cooked through and flakes easily with a fork.

6. Serve hot, garnished with additional lemon slices and fresh herbs.

Health Benefits:

- Fish: Rich in omega-3 fatty acids, which support heart and brain health.

- Herbs: Provide antioxidants and anti-inflammatory properties.

Stewing and Boiling

Stewing and boiling were common methods of cooking in biblical times, often used to prepare soups, stews, and broths.

Biblical Example:

In Genesis 25:29-34, Esau trades his birthright for a bowl of lentil stew prepared by Jacob.

Nutritional Insights:

- Nutrient Preservation: Stewing and boiling help retain the nutrients in the broth, making it a nutritious cooking method.

- Hydration: These methods help maintain the hydration of the food, which can be beneficial for digestion.

Recipe: Lentil and Barley Stew

Ingredients:

- 1 cup dried lentils, rinsed

- ½ cup pearl barley

- 1 onion, chopped

- 2 cloves garlic, minced

- 2 carrots, chopped

- 2 celery stalks, chopped

- 1 can (14.5 oz) diced tomatoes

- 4 cups vegetable broth

- 1 teaspoon ground cumin

- 1 teaspoon ground coriander

- 1 teaspoon dried thyme

- Salt and pepper to taste

- 2 tablespoons olive oil

- Fresh parsley for garnish

Instructions:

1. In a large pot, heat the olive oil over medium heat. Add the onion, garlic, carrots, and celery, and sauté until softened.

2. Add the lentils, barley, diced tomatoes, vegetable broth, cumin, coriander, thyme, salt, and pepper.

3. Bring to a boil, then reduce heat and simmer for about 45 minutes, or until the lentils and barley are tender.

4. Adjust seasoning as needed.

5. Serve hot, garnished with fresh parsley.

Health Benefits:

- Lentils: High in protein, fiber, and iron, promoting muscle repair and digestive health.

- Barley: Rich in fiber, vitamins, and minerals, supporting heart health and digestion.

Baking

Baking is another traditional cooking method that has been used since ancient times, particularly for bread.

Biblical Example:

In Genesis 19:3, Lot prepares a feast that includes unleavened bread for his guests.

Nutritional Insights:

- Whole Grains: Using whole grain flours increases the fiber and nutrient content of baked goods.

- Controlled Ingredients: Baking at home allows for better control over the ingredients, reducing the need for preservatives and additives.

Recipe: Honey and Olive Oil Bread

Ingredients:

- 3 cups whole wheat flour

- 1 cup all-purpose flour

- 2 teaspoons salt

- 2 teaspoons instant yeast

- 1 ½ cups warm water

- ¼ cup honey

- ¼ cup olive oil

Instructions:

1. In a large bowl, mix the whole wheat flour, all-purpose flour, salt, and yeast.

2. In a separate bowl, combine the warm water, honey, and olive oil.

3. Gradually add the wet ingredients to the dry ingredients, mixing until a dough forms.

4. Knead the dough on a floured surface for about 10 minutes, until smooth and elastic.

5. Place the dough in a greased bowl, cover, and let it rise in a warm place for about 1 hour, or until doubled in size.

6. Preheat the oven to 375°F (190°C).

7. Punch down the dough, shape it into a loaf, and place it in a greased loaf pan.

8. Cover and let it rise again for about 30 minutes.

9. Bake for 30-35 minutes, or until the bread sounds hollow when tapped.

10. Let cool before slicing.

Health Benefits:

- Whole Wheat Flour: Rich in fiber, vitamins, and minerals, supporting digestive health and providing sustained energy.

- Honey: Natural sweetener with antibacterial and antioxidant properties.

- Olive Oil: Heart-healthy fats and antioxidants that reduce inflammation.

Fermenting

Fermentation was a common method for preserving food and enhancing its nutritional value in biblical times.

Biblical Example:

Leaven, used in bread making, is a form of fermentation mentioned frequently in the Bible.

Nutritional Insights:

- Probiotics: Fermented foods contain beneficial bacteria that support gut health.

- Nutrient Enhancement: Fermentation can increase the bioavailability of nutrients and improve digestion.

Recipe: Fermented Vegetables

Ingredients:

- 1 medium head cabbage, shredded

- 1 tablespoon sea salt

- 1 carrot, grated

- 1 tablespoon grated ginger

- 2 cloves garlic, minced

- 1 teaspoon caraway seeds (optional)

Instructions:

1. In a large bowl, combine the shredded cabbage and sea salt. Massage the salt into the cabbage until it releases its juices.

2. Add the grated carrot, ginger, garlic, and caraway seeds, and mix well.

3. Pack the mixture tightly into a clean glass jar, pressing down to ensure the cabbage is submerged in its own juices.

4. Cover the jar with a lid and leave it at room temperature to ferment for 5-10 days, tasting periodically until the desired flavor is achieved.

5. Once fermented, store the jar in the refrigerator.

Health Benefits:

- Probiotics: Supports gut health and improves digestion.

- Vitamins and Minerals: Fermentation increases the bioavailability of vitamins and minerals.

Raw Consumption

Eating raw foods, especially fruits and vegetables, was common in biblical times and continues to offer significant health benefits.

Biblical Example:

The consumption of raw fruits, such as figs and pomegranates, is mentioned throughout the Bible.

Nutritional Insights:

- Maximized Nutrients: Raw foods retain all their natural vitamins, minerals, and enzymes, which can be partially lost during cooking.

- Hydration: Many raw fruits and vegetables have high water content, contributing to hydration.

Recipe: Fig and Nut Salad

Ingredients:

- 6 fresh figs, quartered

- 4 cups mixed leafy greens (spinach, arugula, etc.)

- ½ cup walnuts or almonds, toasted

- ¼ cup crumbled goat cheese (optional)

- 2 tablespoons olive oil

- 1 tablespoon balsamic vinegar

- 1 teaspoon honey

- Salt and pepper to taste

Instructions:

1. In a large bowl, combine the mixed greens, figs, and toasted nuts.

2. In a small bowl, whisk together the olive oil, balsamic vinegar, honey, salt, and pepper.

3. Drizzle the dressing over the salad and toss to combine.

4. Top with crumbled goat cheese, if using.

5. Serve immediately.

Health Benefits:

- Figs: High in fiber, vitamins, and minerals, supporting digestive health and bone strength.

- Nuts: Provide healthy fats, protein, and antioxidants.

- Leafy Greens: Rich in vitamins A, C, and K, promoting overall health.

The cooking methods and dietary principles found in the Bible offer a timeless guide to healthy eating. Grilling, roasting, stewing, baking, fermenting, and consuming raw foods provide diverse ways to prepare nutritious meals that align with ancient wisdom. By integrating these methods and biblical ingredients into modern cooking, we can enjoy flavorful, wholesome meals that promote health and well-being. Embracing these practices not only honors the traditions of the past but also enhances our present-day dietary habits, ensuring a balanced and nutritious diet.

Integrating the foods mentioned in the Bible into modern diets can provide numerous health benefits. The cooking methods used in biblical times, combined with contemporary nutritional insights, offer a holistic approach to preparing and enjoying meals. This chapter explores various cooking methods inspired by biblical practices, provides nutritional insights, and includes practical recipes that incorporate these methods and principles.

Cooking Methods

1. Grilling and Roasting

2. Stewing and Boiling

3. Baking

4. Fermenting

5. Raw Consumption

Grilling and Roasting

Grilling and roasting are traditional cooking methods frequently mentioned in the Bible. These techniques not only enhance the flavor of food but also retain essential nutrients.

Biblical Example:

In Genesis 18:6-8, Abraham prepares a meal for his divine guests, which likely included roasted meat.

Nutritional Insights:

- Nutrient Retention: Grilling and roasting at high temperatures help retain water-soluble vitamins (e.g., B vitamins) that can be lost in other cooking methods.

- Flavor Enhancement: These methods enhance the natural flavors of the food without the need for excessive added fats or oils.

Recipe: Grilled Fish with Herbs

Ingredients:

- 4 fish fillets (such as salmon, trout, or tilapia)

- 2 tablespoons olive oil

- 2 cloves garlic, minced

- 1 tablespoon fresh rosemary, chopped

- 1 tablespoon fresh thyme, chopped

- 1 lemon, sliced

- Salt and pepper to taste

Instructions:

1. Preheat the grill to medium-high heat.

2. In a small bowl, combine the olive oil, garlic, rosemary, thyme, salt, and pepper.

3. Brush the fish fillets with the herb mixture.

4. Place the lemon slices on the grill, then place the fish fillets on top of the lemons.

5. Grill for about 4-5 minutes per side, or until the fish is cooked through and flakes easily with a fork.

6. Serve hot, garnished with additional lemon slices and fresh herbs.

Health Benefits:

- Fish: Rich in omega-3 fatty acids, which support heart and brain health.

- Herbs: Provide antioxidants and anti-inflammatory properties.

Stewing and Boiling

Stewing and boiling were common cooking methods in biblical times, often used to prepare soups, stews, and broths.

Biblical Example:

In Genesis 25:29-34, Esau trades his birthright for a bowl of lentil stew prepared by Jacob.

Nutritional Insights:

- Nutrient Preservation: Stewing and boiling help retain nutrients in the broth, making these methods particularly nutritious.

- Hydration: These methods help maintain the hydration of food, which can be beneficial for digestion.

Recipe: Lentil and Barley Stew

Ingredients:

- 1 cup dried lentils, rinsed

- ½ cup pearl barley

- 1 onion, chopped

- 2 cloves garlic, minced

- 2 carrots, chopped

- 2 celery stalks, chopped

- 1 can (14.5 oz) diced tomatoes

- 4 cups vegetable broth

- 1 teaspoon ground cumin

- 1 teaspoon ground coriander

- 1 teaspoon dried thyme

- Salt and pepper to taste

- 2 tablespoons olive oil

- Fresh parsley for garnish

Instructions:

1. In a large pot, heat the olive oil over medium heat. Add the onion, garlic, carrots, and celery, and sauté until softened.

2. Add the lentils, barley, diced tomatoes, vegetable broth, cumin, coriander, thyme, salt, and pepper.

3. Bring to a boil, then reduce heat and simmer for about 45 minutes, or until the lentils and barley are tender.

4. Adjust seasoning as needed.

5. Serve hot, garnished with fresh parsley.

Health Benefits:

- Lentils: High in protein, fiber, and iron, promoting muscle repair and digestive health.

- Barley: Rich in fiber, vitamins, and minerals, supporting heart health and digestion.

Baking

Baking is another traditional cooking method used since ancient times, particularly for bread.

Biblical Example:

In Genesis 19:3, Lot prepares a feast that includes unleavened bread for his guests.

Nutritional Insights:

- Whole Grains: Using whole grain flours increases the fiber and nutrient content of baked goods.

- Controlled Ingredients: Baking at home allows for better control over ingredients, reducing the need for preservatives and additives.

Recipe: Honey and Olive Oil Bread

Ingredients:

- 3 cups whole wheat flour

- 1 cup all-purpose flour

- 2 teaspoons salt

- 2 teaspoons instant yeast

- 1 ½ cups warm water

- ¼ cup honey

- ¼ cup olive oil

Instructions:

1. In a large bowl, mix the whole wheat flour, all-purpose flour, salt, and yeast.

2. In a separate bowl, combine the warm water, honey, and olive oil.

3. Gradually add the wet ingredients to the dry ingredients, mixing until a dough forms.

4. Knead the dough on a floured surface for about 10 minutes, until smooth and elastic.

5. Place the dough in a greased bowl, cover, and let it rise in a warm place for about 1 hour, or until doubled in size.

6. Preheat the oven to 375°F (190°C).

7. Punch down the dough, shape it into a loaf, and place it in a greased loaf pan.

8. Cover and let it rise again for about 30 minutes.

9. Bake for 30-35 minutes, or until the bread sounds hollow when tapped.

10. Let cool before slicing.

Health Benefits:

- Whole Wheat Flour: Rich in fiber, vitamins, and minerals, supporting digestive health and providing sustained energy.

- Honey: Natural sweetener with antibacterial and antioxidant properties.

- Olive Oil: Heart-healthy fats and antioxidants that reduce inflammation.

Fermenting

Fermentation was a common method for preserving food and enhancing its nutritional value in biblical times.

Biblical Example:

Leaven, used in bread making, is a form of fermentation mentioned frequently in the Bible.

Nutritional Insights:

- Probiotics: Fermented foods contain beneficial bacteria that support gut health.

- Nutrient Enhancement: Fermentation can increase the bioavailability of nutrients and improve digestion.

Recipe: Fermented Vegetables

Ingredients:

- 1 medium head cabbage, shredded

- 1 tablespoon sea salt

- 1 carrot, grated

- 1 tablespoon grated ginger

- 2 cloves garlic, minced

- 1 teaspoon caraway seeds (optional)

Instructions:

1. In a large bowl, combine the shredded cabbage and sea salt. Massage the salt into the cabbage until it releases its juices.

2. Add the grated carrot, ginger, garlic, and caraway seeds, and mix well.

3. Pack the mixture tightly into a clean glass jar, pressing down to ensure the cabbage is submerged in its own juices.

4. Cover the jar with a lid and leave it at room temperature to ferment for 5-10 days, tasting periodically until the desired flavor is achieved.

5. Once fermented, store the jar in the refrigerator.

Health Benefits:

- Probiotics: Supports gut health and improves digestion.

- Vitamins and Minerals: Fermentation increases the bioavailability of vitamins and minerals.

Raw Consumption

Eating raw foods, especially fruits and vegetables, was common in biblical times and continues to offer significant health benefits.

Biblical Example:

The consumption of raw fruits, such as figs and pomegranates, is mentioned throughout the Bible.

Nutritional Insights:

- Maximized Nutrients: Raw foods retain all their natural vitamins, minerals, and enzymes, which can be partially lost during cooking.

- Hydration: Many raw fruits and vegetables have high water content, contributing to hydration.

Recipe: Fig and Nut Salad

Ingredients:

- 6 fresh figs, quartered

- 4 cups mixed leafy greens (spinach, arugula, etc.)

- ½ cup walnuts or almonds, toasted

- ¼ cup crumbled goat cheese (optional)

- 2 tablespoons olive oil

- 1 tablespoon balsamic vinegar

- 1 teaspoon honey

- Salt and pepper to taste

Instructions:

1. In a large bowl, combine the mixed greens, figs, and toasted nuts.

2. In a small bowl, whisk together the olive oil, balsamic vinegar, honey, salt, and pepper.

3. Drizzle the dressing over the salad and toss to combine.

4. Top with crumbled goat cheese, if using.

5. Serve immediately.

Health Benefits:

- Figs: High in fiber, vitamins, and minerals, supporting digestive health and bone strength.

- Nuts: Provide healthy fats, protein, and antioxidants.

- Leafy Greens: Rich in vitamins A, C, and K, promoting overall health.

The cooking methods and dietary principles found in the Bible offer a timeless guide to healthy eating. Grilling, roasting, stewing, baking, fermenting, and consuming raw foods provide diverse ways to prepare nutritious meals that align with ancient wisdom. By integrating these methods and biblical ingredients into modern cooking, we can enjoy flavorful, wholesome meals that promote health and well-being. Embracing these practices not only honors the traditions of the past but also enhances our present-day dietary habits, ensuring a balanced and nutritious diet.

CHAPTER 07

SPIRITUAL DIMENSIONS OF FOOD

The Bible uses food not only as a source of physical sustenance but also as a powerful symbol of spiritual truths. Throughout the Scriptures, food is imbued with deep spiritual significance, reflecting themes of provision, fellowship, sacrifice, and divine revelation. This chapter explores the spiritual dimensions of food in the Bible, examining how various foods symbolize and convey profound theological messages.

Bread: Symbol of Life and Provision

Bread is one of the most frequently mentioned foods in the Bible, symbolizing God's provision and the sustenance of life. It appears in numerous contexts, from the manna in the wilderness to the Last Supper, underscoring its central role in both daily life and spiritual symbolism.

Manna in the Wilderness:

In Exodus 16, God provides manna, a miraculous bread from heaven, to sustain the Israelites during their journey through the desert.

Exodus 16:4: "Then the Lord said to Moses, 'I will rain down bread from heaven for you. The people are to go out each day and gather enough for that day.'"

Manna symbolizes God's direct provision and care for His people, teaching them to rely on Him daily.

The Bread of Life:

In the New Testament, Jesus declares Himself to be the Bread of Life, connecting the physical sustenance of bread with spiritual nourishment.

John 6:35: "Then Jesus declared, 'I am the bread of life. Whoever comes to me will never go hungry, and whoever believes in me will never be thirsty.'"

This declaration highlights Jesus as the essential source of spiritual life and fulfillment, offering eternal sustenance to those who believe in Him.

The Last Supper:

During the Last Supper, Jesus breaks bread and shares it with His disciples, instituting the Eucharist.

Matthew 26:26: "While they were eating, Jesus took bread, and when he had given thanks, he broke it and gave it to his disciples, saying, 'Take and eat; this is my body.'"

The breaking of bread in the Eucharist symbolizes Jesus' sacrifice and His presence with believers, providing spiritual nourishment and unity.

Wine: Symbol of Joy and Sacrifice

Wine is another significant symbol in the Bible, representing joy, blessing, and the blood of Christ.

Joy and Celebration:

Wine is often associated with joy and celebration in biblical times. It was a staple at feasts and weddings, symbolizing God's blessings and the abundance of life.

Psalm 104:15: "Wine that gladdens human hearts, oil to make their faces shine, and bread that sustains their hearts."

The Blood of the Covenant:

At the Last Supper, Jesus uses wine to symbolize His blood, shed for the forgiveness of sins.

Matthew 26:27-28: "Then he took a cup, and when he had given thanks, he gave it to them, saying, 'Drink from it, all of you. This is my blood of the covenant, which is poured out for many for the forgiveness of sins.'"

This act establishes wine as a powerful symbol of Jesus' sacrificial death and the new covenant between God and humanity.

The Wedding at Cana:

Jesus' first miracle, turning water into wine at the wedding in Cana, signifies the transformative power of His ministry and the joy of the new covenant.

John 2:10: "Everyone brings out the choice wine first and then the cheaper wine after the guests have had too much to drink, but you have saved the best till now."

This miracle illustrates the abundance and excellence of the new life Jesus brings.

Fruits: Symbols of Abundance and Spiritual Fruitfulness

Fruits in the Bible often symbolize abundance, blessing, and the results of a life lived in accordance with God's will.

The Promised Land:

The land promised to the Israelites is frequently described as a land flowing with milk and honey, indicating its fertility and abundance.

Deuteronomy 8:8: "A land with wheat and barley, vines and fig trees, pomegranates, olive oil and honey."

These fruits symbolize the richness of God's provision and the blessings of living in obedience to Him.

Spiritual Fruitfulness:

In the New Testament, fruits are used metaphorically to describe the virtues and behaviors that result from living a life guided by the Holy Spirit.

Galatians 5:22-23: "But the fruit of the Spirit is love, joy, peace, forbearance, kindness, goodness, faithfulness, gentleness and self-control."

These spiritual fruits are the visible manifestations of a life transformed by God's presence and power.

Milk and Honey: Symbols of Promise and Prosperity

Milk and honey are frequently mentioned together in the Bible, symbolizing prosperity, nourishment, and the fulfillment of God's promises.

The Promised Land:

The description of the Promised Land as flowing with milk and honey represents the abundance and prosperity that God has prepared for His people.

Exodus 3:8: "So I have come down to rescue them from the hand of the Egyptians and to bring them up out of that land into a good and spacious land, a land flowing with milk and honey."

This imagery conveys the idea of a bountiful and fertile land, emphasizing God's generous provision.

Spiritual Nourishment:

Milk, as a basic and essential food, also symbolizes the nourishing and sustaining power of God's word.

1 Peter 2:2: "Like newborn babies, crave pure spiritual milk, so that by it you may grow up in your salvation."

This metaphor highlights the importance of spiritual nourishment for growth and maturity in the faith.

Olive Oil: Symbol of Anointing and Healing

Olive oil is a significant symbol in the Bible, representing anointing, healing, and the presence of the Holy Spirit.

Anointing Kings and Priests:

Olive oil was used to anoint kings and priests, signifying their consecration and the presence of God's Spirit upon them.

1 Samuel 16:13: "So Samuel took the horn of oil and anointed him in the presence of his brothers, and from that day on the Spirit of the Lord came powerfully upon David."

Healing:

Olive oil was also used for its healing properties, as seen in the parable of the Good Samaritan.

Luke 10:34: "He went to him and bandaged his wounds, pouring on oil and wine."

This act of compassion and healing symbolizes the restorative power of God's love and care.

Symbol of the Holy Spirit:

Olive oil often represents the Holy Spirit's presence and anointing in a believer's life.

1 John 2:20: "But you have an anointing from the Holy One, and all of you know the truth."

This spiritual anointing empowers believers for service and signifies their relationship with God.

The Table: Symbol of Fellowship and Communion

The table, where food is shared, is a powerful symbol of fellowship, community, and communion with God and others.

The Lord's Table:

The Lord's Table, or Communion, is a central act of worship in Christianity, symbolizing the believers' fellowship with Christ and each other.

1 Corinthians 10:16-17: "Is not the cup of thanksgiving for which we give thanks a participation in the blood of Christ? And is not the bread that we break a participation in the body of Christ? Because there is one loaf, we, who are many, are one body, for we all share the one loaf."

This act of sharing a meal symbolizes unity, forgiveness, and the spiritual nourishment received from Christ.

Feasting in the Kingdom:

The Bible often uses the imagery of a banquet or feast to describe the joy and fellowship of God's Kingdom.

Isaiah 25:6: "On this mountain, the Lord Almighty will prepare a feast of rich food for all peoples, a banquet of aged wine—the best of meats and the finest of wines."

This imagery conveys the abundance, joy, and fellowship that characterize the Kingdom of God.

The spiritual symbolism of food in the Bible adds profound depth to our understanding of God's provision, fellowship, and salvation. Bread, wine, fruits, milk and honey, olive oil, and the table each carry rich spiritual meanings that transcend their physical forms, pointing to deeper theological truths about God's relationship with humanity. By recognizing and reflecting on these symbols, believers can gain a greater appreciation for the ways in which everyday sustenance connects to the divine, enriching both their physical and spiritual lives.

How Food Can Be a Tool for Spiritual Growth and Well-being

Food, while essential for physical nourishment, also plays a crucial role in spiritual growth and well-being. Throughout the Bible, food is used as a metaphor for spiritual truths, a medium for fellowship, and a means of cultivating discipline and gratitude. This chapter explores how food can be a tool for enhancing one's spiritual life, fostering community, and deepening one's relationship with God.

The Role of Food in Spiritual Practices

1. Fasting: A Discipline of Denial

2. Feasting: A Celebration of God's Goodness

3. Communion: A Sacrament of Remembrance

4. Hospitality: A Practice of Generosity

Fasting: A Discipline of Denial

Fasting, the voluntary abstention from food, is a spiritual discipline practiced throughout the Bible. It serves as a powerful tool for spiritual growth, helping believers focus on their relationship with God and develop self-control.

Biblical Example:

Jesus fasted for forty days in the wilderness, using this time to prepare for His public ministry and to overcome temptation.

Matthew 4:1-2: "Then Jesus was led by the Spirit into the wilderness to be tempted by the devil. After fasting forty days and forty nights, he was hungry."

Spiritual Benefits:

- Increased Focus on God: Fasting creates space to draw closer to God, removing distractions and fostering deeper spiritual awareness.

- Self-Discipline: Abstaining from food cultivates self-control and strengthens the will, helping believers resist temptation in other areas of life.

- Repentance and Humility: Fasting is often associated with repentance and humility, acknowledging dependence on God for sustenance and strength.

Practical Application:

- Regular Fasting: Integrate regular fasting into your spiritual routine, whether it's skipping a meal, fasting for a day, or practicing intermittent fasting.

- Spiritual Focus: Use fasting periods for prayer, meditation, and reading Scripture, redirecting the time and energy usually spent on eating towards spiritual growth.

Feasting: A Celebration of God's Goodness

Feasting is an essential aspect of biblical tradition, celebrating God's provision and the joy of community. It serves as a reminder of God's blessings and an opportunity to express gratitude.

Biblical Example:

The Israelites celebrated several feasts, such as Passover and the Feast of Tabernacles, to commemorate God's faithfulness and deliverance.

Deuteronomy 16:14-15: "Be joyful at your festival—you, your sons and daughters, your male and female servants, and the Levites, the foreigners, the fatherless and the widows who live in your towns. For seven days celebrate the festival to the Lord your God at the place the Lord will choose. For the Lord your God will bless you in all your harvest and in all the work of your hands, and your joy will be complete."

Spiritual Benefits:

- Gratitude: Feasting fosters a sense of gratitude, recognizing God's provision and generosity.

- Community: Sharing meals strengthens bonds within the community, promoting fellowship and unity.

- Remembrance: Feasts serve as reminders of God's past faithfulness, reinforcing trust in His continued provision.

Practical Application:

- Celebrate Holy Days: Observe biblical feasts or Christian holidays with special meals, reflecting on their spiritual significance.

- Gratitude Practices: Begin meals with prayers of thanksgiving, acknowledging God's provision.

- Community Meals: Host regular gatherings with family, friends, or church members to share meals and build relationships.

Communion: A Sacrament of Remembrance

The act of Communion, also known as the Lord's Supper, is a central practice in Christianity, symbolizing Jesus' sacrifice and fostering spiritual unity among believers.

Biblical Example:

Jesus instituted Communion during the Last Supper, instructing His disciples to remember His sacrifice through the breaking of bread and sharing of wine.

Luke 22:19-20: "And he took bread, gave thanks and broke it, and gave it to them, saying, 'This is my body given for you; do this in remembrance of me.' In the same way, after the supper he took the cup, saying, 'This cup is the new covenant in my blood, which is poured out for you.'"

Spiritual Benefits:

- Remembrance: Communion is a tangible reminder of Jesus' sacrifice, fostering gratitude and reverence.

- Unity: Sharing Communion unites believers, reinforcing the bond of faith and community.

- Reflection: The sacrament encourages self-examination and repentance, promoting spiritual growth and renewal.

Practical Application:

- Regular Participation: Participate in Communion regularly, whether in a church setting or at home with family.

- Reflective Practice: Approach Communion with a reflective heart, meditating on the significance of Jesus' sacrifice and the new covenant.

- Community Involvement: Use Communion as an opportunity to strengthen relationships within your faith community.

Hospitality: A Practice of Generosity

Hospitality, the act of welcoming and providing for others, is a significant theme in the Bible. Sharing food with others is a practical expression of love, generosity, and service.

Biblical Example:

Abraham's hospitality to three divine visitors illustrates the importance of welcoming others and providing for their needs.

Genesis 18:1-8: "Abraham looked up and saw three men standing nearby. When he saw them, he hurried from the entrance of his tent to meet them and bowed low to the ground. He said, 'If I have found favor in your eyes, my lord, do not pass your servant by. Let a little water be brought, and then you may all wash your feet and rest under this tree. Let me get you something to eat, so you can be refreshed and then go on your way—now that you have come to your servant.'"

Spiritual Benefits:

- Generosity: Practicing hospitality fosters a spirit of generosity and selflessness.

- Service: Providing food for others is a tangible way to serve and bless those around you.

- Connection: Sharing meals with guests builds relationships and creates opportunities for spiritual conversations and encouragement.

Practical Application:

- Open Your Home: Regularly invite friends, neighbors, or church members for meals, creating a welcoming environment.

- Serve Others: Look for opportunities to provide meals for those in need, such as new parents, the sick, or the elderly.

- Community Outreach: Use hospitality as a means of outreach, inviting others to experience the love and fellowship of your faith community.

Food as a Metaphor for Spiritual Nourishment

Food is frequently used as a metaphor for spiritual nourishment in the Bible, illustrating the importance of feeding on God's word and finding sustenance in Him.

Biblical Example:

Jesus refers to Himself as the Bread of Life, emphasizing the necessity of spiritual sustenance.

John 6:35: "Then Jesus declared, 'I am the bread of life. Whoever comes to me will never go hungry, and whoever believes in me will never be thirsty.'"

Spiritual Benefits:

- Spiritual Growth: Just as food nourishes the body, God's word nourishes the soul, promoting spiritual growth and maturity.

- Satisfaction: Finding satisfaction in God prevents spiritual hunger and thirst, leading to a fulfilling and abundant life.

- Wisdom: Feeding on God's word provides wisdom, guidance, and strength for daily living.

Practical Application:

- Daily Devotions: Make time for daily Bible reading and prayer, feeding on God's word for spiritual nourishment.

- Scripture Meditation: Reflect on Scripture passages, allowing them to permeate your heart and mind.

- Spiritual Study: Engage in deeper study of the Bible, seeking to understand its truths and apply them to your life.

Food, as presented in the Bible, serves as a powerful tool for spiritual growth and well-being. Through practices like fasting, feasting, Communion, and hospitality, believers can deepen their relationship with God, foster community, and cultivate a spirit of gratitude and service. By recognizing the spiritual dimensions of food and incorporating these practices into daily life, believers can experience the fullness of God's provision and the richness of a life lived in communion with Him. Embracing these spiritual aspects of food not only nourishes the body but also feeds the soul, leading to a more holistic and fulfilling spiritual journey.

CHAPTER 08

INTEGRATING BIBLICAL WISDOM INTO MODERN LIFE

Incorporating the timeless wisdom of biblical dietary principles into modern life can significantly enhance our physical and spiritual well-being. This chapter offers practical tips for integrating these ancient guidelines into contemporary diets, ensuring that we honor both our health and our faith.

Embrace Whole, Natural Foods

One of the core principles of biblical nutrition is the emphasis on whole, natural foods. By prioritizing these foods, we can benefit from their full nutritional value and avoid the health risks associated with processed foods.

Practical Tips:

- Choose Whole Grains: Opt for whole grains like barley, wheat, quinoa, and brown rice instead of refined grains. Whole grains retain more nutrients and fiber, supporting digestive health and providing sustained energy.

- Incorporate Fresh Fruits and Vegetables: Include a variety of fresh fruits and vegetables in your diet. Aim for a colorful plate to ensure a wide range of vitamins, minerals, and antioxidants.

- Select Lean Proteins: Favor lean protein sources such as fish, poultry, legumes, and nuts. These options provide essential nutrients without the unhealthy fats found in processed meats.

- Use Natural Sweeteners: Replace refined sugars with natural sweeteners like honey or maple syrup. These options offer additional health benefits, such as antibacterial properties in honey.

Recipe: Quinoa and Vegetable Salad

Ingredients:

- 1 cup quinoa, rinsed

- 2 cups water

- 1 cucumber, diced

- 1 bell pepper, diced

- 1 cup cherry tomatoes, halved

- 1/4 cup red onion, finely chopped

- 1/4 cup fresh parsley, chopped

- 1/4 cup fresh mint, chopped

- 2 tablespoons olive oil

- 1 tablespoon lemon juice

- Salt and pepper to taste

Instructions:

1. In a medium saucepan, bring the quinoa and water to a boil. Reduce heat, cover, and simmer for 15 minutes, or until the quinoa is cooked and water is absorbed. Fluff with a fork and let cool.

2. In a large bowl, combine the cooked quinoa, cucumber, bell pepper, cherry tomatoes, red onion, parsley, and mint.

3. In a small bowl, whisk together the olive oil, lemon juice, salt, and pepper.

4. Pour the dressing over the salad and toss to combine.

5. Serve chilled or at room temperature.

Health Benefits:

- Quinoa: High in protein, fiber, and essential amino acids, promoting muscle health and digestion.

- Vegetables: Provide a rich array of vitamins, minerals, and antioxidants.

Practice Moderation and Balance

Biblical principles advocate for moderation and balance in eating habits, warning against gluttony and overindulgence.

Practical Tips:

- Mindful Eating: Pay attention to hunger and fullness cues. Eat slowly and savor each bite to avoid overeating.

- Portion Control: Serve appropriate portions to prevent overeating. Use smaller plates if necessary to help control portion sizes.

- Balanced Meals: Ensure that each meal includes a balance of macronutrients (proteins, fats, and carbohydrates) and a variety of foods from different food groups.

Recipe: Balanced Mediterranean Plate

Ingredients:

- 1 cup cooked quinoa or brown rice

- 1/2 cup hummus

- 1/2 cup cherry tomatoes, halved

- 1/2 cucumber, sliced

- 1/4 cup olives

- 1/4 cup feta cheese, crumbled

- 2 tablespoons olive oil

- 1 tablespoon lemon juice

- Salt and pepper to taste

Instructions:

1. Arrange the quinoa or brown rice on a plate.

2. Add the hummus, cherry tomatoes, cucumber, olives, and feta cheese.

3. Drizzle with olive oil and lemon juice.

4. Season with salt and pepper.

5. Serve as a balanced meal.

Health Benefits:

- Quinoa/Brown Rice: Provide complex carbohydrates and fiber for sustained energy.

- Hummus: Offers plant-based protein and healthy fats.

- Vegetables: Supply essential vitamins and minerals.

Observe Fasting and Feasting

Fasting and feasting are important spiritual practices in the Bible that can also contribute to physical health.

Practical Tips:

- Regular Fasting: Incorporate intermittent fasting into your routine, such as fasting for 16 hours and eating within an 8-hour window. This practice can help with weight management, metabolic health, and spiritual discipline.

- Celebratory Feasting: Mark special occasions with celebratory meals that include loved ones. Use these times to reflect on God's blessings and foster community.

Recipe: Festive Lentil Stew for Feasting

Ingredients:

- 1 cup lentils, rinsed

- 1 onion, chopped

- 2 cloves garlic, minced

- 2 carrots, chopped

- 2 celery stalks, chopped

- 1 can diced tomatoes

- 4 cups vegetable broth

- 1 teaspoon ground cumin

- 1 teaspoon ground coriander

- 1 teaspoon dried thyme

- 2 tablespoons olive oil

- Salt and pepper to taste

- Fresh parsley for garnish

Instructions:

1. In a large pot, heat the olive oil over medium heat. Add the onion, garlic, carrots, and celery, and sauté until softened.

2. Add the lentils, diced tomatoes, vegetable broth, cumin, coriander, thyme, salt, and pepper.

3. Bring to a boil, then reduce heat and simmer for about 45 minutes, or until the lentils are tender.

4. Adjust seasoning as needed.

5. Serve hot, garnished with fresh parsley.

Health Benefits:

- Lentils: Rich in protein, fiber, and iron, supporting muscle repair and digestive health.

- Vegetables: Provide a range of essential nutrients and antioxidants.

Embrace Hospitality

Hospitality is a key biblical principle that involves sharing food and providing for others, fostering community and fellowship.

Practical Tips:

- Invite Others: Regularly invite friends, neighbors, or church members for meals. Use these occasions to build relationships and share your faith.

- Serve with Love: Prepare meals with care and serve them with a spirit of generosity and hospitality.

- Community Outreach: Participate in community meals or provide food for those in need as an act of service.

Recipe: Simple and Nutritious Hospitality Meal

Ingredients:

- 4 chicken breasts

- 2 tablespoons olive oil

- 2 cloves garlic, minced

- 1 teaspoon dried oregano

- 1 teaspoon dried thyme

- Salt and pepper to taste

- 1 lemon, sliced

- 4 cups mixed salad greens

- 1 cup cherry tomatoes, halved

- 1 cucumber, sliced

- 1/4 cup red onion, thinly sliced

Instructions:

1. Preheat the oven to 375°F (190°C).

2. In a baking dish, place the chicken breasts and drizzle with olive oil.

3. Sprinkle with garlic, oregano, thyme, salt, and pepper.

4. Arrange lemon slices on top of the chicken.

5. Bake for 25-30 minutes, or until the chicken is cooked through.

6. Meanwhile, prepare the salad by combining the mixed greens, cherry tomatoes, cucumber, and red onion in a large bowl.

7. Serve the chicken with the fresh salad on the side.

Health Benefits:

- Chicken: Provides lean protein essential for muscle maintenance and repair.

- Salad: Offers a variety of vitamins, minerals, and antioxidants.

Seek Spiritual Nourishment

Integrating biblical principles into your diet goes beyond physical health; it also involves seeking spiritual nourishment through food-related practices.

Practical Tips:

- Prayer and Meditation: Begin each meal with a prayer of thanksgiving, acknowledging God's provision and asking for His blessing on the food.

- Scripture Reflection: Reflect on biblical passages that relate to food and nourishment, considering how they apply to your life.

- Gratitude Journaling: Keep a journal of gratitude, noting how God's provision through food sustains and blesses you each day.

Recipe: Grateful Heart Breakfast Bowl

Ingredients:

- 1 cup cooked oatmeal

- 1 banana, sliced

- 1/4 cup blueberries

- 1 tablespoon chia seeds

- 1 tablespoon almond butter

- 1 teaspoon honey

- 1/4 teaspoon cinnamon

Instructions:

1. Prepare the oatmeal according to package instructions.

2. Top with banana slices, blueberries, chia seeds, almond butter, honey, and a sprinkle of cinnamon.

3. Serve warm and enjoy with a grateful heart.

Health Benefits:

- Oatmeal: High in fiber and provides sustained energy.

- Fruits: Rich in vitamins, minerals, and antioxidants.

- Chia Seeds and Almond Butter: Provide healthy fats and protein.

Integrating biblical wisdom into modern life involves embracing whole, natural foods, practicing moderation and balance, observing fasting and feasting, extending hospitality, and seeking spiritual nourishment. These practices not only enhance physical health but also deepen spiritual well-being, fostering a holistic approach to food and health. By following these practical tips and incorporating biblical principles into your daily diet, you can honor your body as a temple of the Holy Spirit and live a life that reflects gratitude, generosity, and reverence for God's provision.

Challenges and Benefits of Adopting a Biblical Diet

Adopting a biblical diet, grounded in the principles and foods mentioned in the Scriptures, offers numerous physical and spiritual benefits. However, integrating these ancient dietary guidelines into modern life can also present certain challenges. This chapter explores both the challenges and benefits of embracing a biblical diet, providing practical strategies to overcome obstacles and fully enjoy the advantages of this holistic approach to eating.

Challenges of Adopting a Biblical Diet

1. Accessibility and Availability of Foods

2. Cultural and Dietary Preferences

3. Modern Food Industry Influences

4. Social and Family Dynamics

5. Understanding and Interpreting Biblical Guidelines

Accessibility and Availability of Foods

Challenge:

Some foods mentioned in the Bible may not be readily available in all regions or may be more expensive compared to processed alternatives. Ingredients like figs, dates, and certain types of fish may be seasonal or imported, impacting their accessibility.

Strategies to Overcome:

- Local Alternatives: Identify and use locally available foods that have similar nutritional profiles. For example, substitute locally available fruits for biblical fruits like figs or dates.

- Seasonal Eating: Focus on consuming seasonal produce to ensure freshness and affordability.

- Bulk Purchasing: Buy non-perishable biblical foods like grains, nuts, and seeds in bulk to reduce costs.

Cultural and Dietary Preferences

Challenge:

Modern diets often include foods and preparation methods that differ significantly from those in biblical times. Transitioning to a biblical diet may require significant changes in eating habits and preferences.

Strategies to Overcome:

- Gradual Transition: Make incremental changes to your diet rather than drastic shifts. Start by incorporating one or two biblical foods or meals each week.

- Recipe Adaptation: Adapt familiar recipes to include biblical ingredients, making the transition smoother and more enjoyable.

- Cultural Fusion: Blend biblical dietary principles with your cultural food traditions to create meals that respect both biblical guidelines and cultural preferences.

Modern Food Industry Influences

Challenge:

The modern food industry heavily promotes processed and convenience foods, which can be challenging to avoid. These foods often contain additives, preservatives, and unhealthy fats that are inconsistent with a biblical diet.

Strategies to Overcome:

- Education and Awareness: Educate yourself about the ingredients and nutritional content of the foods you consume. Read labels carefully and choose whole, minimally processed foods.

- Home Cooking: Prioritize cooking meals at home using fresh, natural ingredients. This allows greater control over what goes into your food.

- Meal Planning: Plan your meals and snacks ahead of time to avoid the temptation of convenience foods. Prepare and store healthy options for busy days.

Social and Family Dynamics

Challenge:

Adopting a biblical diet may be challenging in social settings or within families where others do not share the same dietary practices. This can lead to feelings of isolation or difficulty in maintaining the diet.

Strategies to Overcome:

- Communication: Communicate your dietary choices with family and friends, explaining the reasons behind your decisions and seeking their support.

- Shared Meals: Involve family members in meal planning and preparation. Find common ground by preparing meals that everyone can enjoy, incorporating biblical foods where possible.

- Flexibility: Be flexible in social situations. When dining out or attending gatherings, focus on making the best possible choices within the available options and maintaining balance.

Understanding and Interpreting Biblical Guidelines

Challenge:

Interpreting and understanding biblical dietary guidelines can be complex, especially given the historical and cultural context of the Scriptures. This can lead to confusion about what foods to include or exclude.

Strategies to Overcome:

- Study and Research: Invest time in studying the Bible and related resources to gain a deeper understanding of biblical dietary principles. Seek out reputable sources and consider consulting with knowledgeable individuals or groups.

- Simplification: Focus on the core principles of a biblical diet, such as consuming whole, natural foods, practicing moderation, and fostering gratitude and community.

- Seek Guidance: Join a faith-based group or community that shares an interest in biblical nutrition. Sharing experiences and knowledge can provide support and clarity.

Benefits of Adopting a Biblical Diet

1. Improved Physical Health

2. Enhanced Spiritual Well-being

3. Strengthened Community and Relationships

4. Sustainable and Ethical Eating

Improved Physical Health

Benefit:

A biblical diet emphasizes whole, natural foods, which are rich in essential nutrients and free from harmful additives. This approach promotes overall health and can prevent chronic diseases.

Examples:

- Increased Nutrient Intake: Whole grains, fruits, vegetables, nuts, and seeds provide a wide range of vitamins, minerals, and antioxidants.

- Reduced Disease Risk: Consuming lean proteins, healthy fats, and fiber-rich foods can lower the risk of heart disease, diabetes, and certain cancers.

- Weight Management: A focus on natural, unprocessed foods supports healthy weight management and reduces the risk of obesity.

Enhanced Spiritual Well-being

Benefit:

Following a biblical diet fosters a deeper connection with God by aligning daily practices with spiritual principles. This intentional approach to eating can enhance spiritual growth and mindfulness.

Examples:

- Mindful Eating: Practicing gratitude and mindfulness during meals fosters a sense of spiritual awareness and appreciation for God's provision.

- Spiritual Disciplines: Incorporating fasting and feasting as spiritual disciplines strengthens one's faith and reliance on God.

- Holistic Health: Recognizing the body as a temple of the Holy Spirit encourages caring for one's physical health as part of spiritual stewardship.

Strengthened Community and Relationships

Benefit:

Sharing meals and practicing hospitality is central to a biblical diet, fostering deeper connections with others and building a sense of community.

Examples:

- Hospitality: Opening your home and sharing meals with others cultivates generosity and strengthens relationships.

- Community Building: Participating in communal meals and celebrations promotes unity and fellowship within faith communities.

- Support Systems: Engaging with others who share similar dietary practices provides mutual support and encouragement.

Sustainable and Ethical Eating

Benefit:

A biblical diet often aligns with principles of sustainability and ethical eating, emphasizing stewardship of the earth and compassionate treatment of animals.

Examples:

- Sustainable Choices: Prioritizing locally sourced, seasonal, and organic foods reduces environmental impact and supports local farmers.

- Ethical Practices: Consuming plant-based foods and ethically raised animals aligns with principles of compassion and stewardship.

- Reduced Waste: Focusing on whole foods and home-cooked meals minimizes food waste and reliance on disposable packaging.

Adopting a biblical diet offers numerous benefits for physical health, spiritual well-being, community building, and sustainable living. While challenges such as accessibility, cultural preferences, and modern food industry influences may arise, practical strategies can help overcome these obstacles. By embracing the core principles of a biblical diet and integrating them into daily life, individuals can experience the profound advantages of this holistic approach to eating, honoring both their bodies and their faith.

CONCLUSION

The exploration of healing foods in the Bible reveals a profound and enduring wisdom that extends beyond mere sustenance. The Bible's dietary practices encompass physical health, spiritual well-being, community building, and ethical living, offering a holistic approach to nourishment that remains relevant today. This conclusion summarizes the key takeaways and reflects on the timeless nature of biblical dietary principles.

Key Takeaways

1. Emphasis on Whole, Natural Foods:

- The Bible promotes the consumption of whole, unprocessed foods, such as grains, fruits, vegetables, nuts, and seeds. These foods are rich in essential nutrients and support overall health and well-being.

- Examples: Barley, wheat, figs, grapes, pomegranates, olives, honey.

2. Balance and Moderation:

- Biblical principles advocate for balanced eating habits and moderation, warning against gluttony and overindulgence. This promotes a healthy relationship with food and supports physical and spiritual health.

- Practices: Mindful eating, portion control, balanced meals.

3. Spiritual Significance of Food:

- Food in the Bible often carries spiritual symbolism, representing divine provision, fellowship, and sacrifice. Practices like fasting, feasting, and Communion deepen one's spiritual connection and awareness.

- Symbols: Bread (life and provision), wine (joy and sacrifice), fruits (abundance and spiritual fruitfulness), milk and honey (prosperity).

4. Healing Properties:

- Many foods mentioned in the Bible have healing properties validated by modern science. These include honey's antibacterial effects, olive oil's heart health benefits, and the digestive support provided by figs and lentils.

- Healing Foods: Honey, olive oil, figs, lentils, garlic, herbs and spices.

5. Community and Fellowship:

- Sharing meals is a significant aspect of biblical teachings, fostering community, hospitality, and mutual support. This practice strengthens relationships and builds a sense of belonging.

- Practices: Hospitality, communal meals, feasting.

6. Sustainable and Ethical Eating:

- Biblical dietary practices align with principles of sustainability and ethical living, emphasizing stewardship of the earth and compassionate treatment of animals.

- Practices: Locally sourced foods, plant-based eating, ethical treatment of animals.

Final Thoughts on the Enduring Wisdom of Biblical Dietary Practices

The enduring wisdom of biblical dietary practices lies in their holistic approach to health and well-being. These practices recognize the interconnectedness of physical nourishment, spiritual growth, and community life, offering a comprehensive guide to living a balanced and fulfilling life.

Timeless Relevance:

Despite the passage of centuries, the principles found in the Bible continue to provide valuable insights for modern living. The emphasis on whole foods, moderation, and mindful eating aligns closely with contemporary nutritional science, validating the health benefits of these ancient practices.

Holistic Health:

Biblical dietary guidelines promote a holistic view of health that integrates body, mind, and spirit. By following these principles, individuals can achieve not only physical well-being but also spiritual fulfillment and a deeper sense of purpose.

Community and Connection:

The Bible's focus on communal meals and hospitality underscores the importance of relationships and community support. These practices foster a sense of belonging and mutual care, which are essential for emotional and social well-being.

Ethical and Sustainable Living:

Embracing biblical dietary practices encourages sustainable and ethical choices, reflecting a commitment to caring for the earth and its creatures. This aligns with modern movements towards sustainability and ethical consumption.

In conclusion, the healing foods and dietary principles outlined in the Bible offer a rich tapestry of wisdom that can guide us towards a healthier, more balanced, and spiritually enriched life. By integrating these timeless practices into our modern lives, we honor the profound connection between our physical sustenance and our spiritual journey, fostering a holistic approach to living that nourishes both body and soul.

APPENDIX

This appendix provides additional resources, references, and further reading materials for those interested in exploring the topics of biblical dietary practices, healing foods, and their integration into modern life. These resources offer deeper insights, practical advice, and scholarly perspectives to enhance your understanding and application of the principles discussed in this book.

Books and Publications

1. "The Maker's Diet" by Jordan S. Rubin

   - A comprehensive guide that explores the connection between faith and health, offering dietary advice based on biblical principles and modern nutritional science.

2. "What Would Jesus Eat?: The Ultimate Program for Eating Well, Feeling Great, and Living Longer" by Don Colbert

- This book examines the diet of Jesus and provides practical guidelines for adopting a similar eating plan for improved health and well-being.

3. "Food in the Bible: From Adam's Apple to the Last Supper" by Leola S. Brooks

- An exploration of the significance of food in biblical times, including cultural, historical, and spiritual perspectives.

4. "Healing Foods of the Bible" by Bernard Ward

- This book details various foods mentioned in the Bible, their health benefits, and how to incorporate them into a modern diet.

5. "The Daniel Plan: 40 Days to a Healthier Life" by Rick Warren, Daniel Amen, and Mark Hyman

- A program that combines faith, food, fitness, focus, and friends to promote holistic health based on biblical principles.

Academic Articles and Journals

1. "Biblical Nutrition: Implications for the Contemporary Believer" - Journal of Religion and Health

- An academic article that discusses the nutritional principles found in the Bible and their relevance to modern dietary practices.

2. "Ancient Grains: A Biblical Perspective on Modern Health" - Journal of Biblical Literature

- This paper explores the role of ancient grains in biblical diets and their health benefits in contemporary nutrition.

3. "The Role of Fasting in Biblical Tradition and Modern Health" - Journal of Fasting and Health

- An analysis of the spiritual and physical benefits of fasting as practiced in biblical times and its applications today.

Online Resources and Websites

1. Bible Gateway (www.biblegateway.com)

- An online Bible study tool with various translations and resources for exploring biblical texts related to food and health.

2. Blue Letter Bible (www.blueletterbible.org)

- A comprehensive online resource for studying the Bible, including commentaries, dictionaries, and concordances.

3. The Daniel Plan (www.danielplan.com)

- A website offering resources, recipes, and community support for those following The Daniel Plan for holistic health.

4. The Maker's Diet (www.makersdiet.com)

- A resource site for those interested in Jordan Rubin's approach to biblical nutrition and health.

5. Weston A. Price Foundation (www.westonaprice.org)

- Provides information on traditional diets, including biblical foods and their health benefits.

Cooking and Recipe Resources

1. "Feasts of the Bible Cookbook" by Mindy Montgomery

- A cookbook that offers recipes inspired by biblical feasts and foods, along with historical and cultural insights.

2. "The Biblical Nutritionist" (www.thebiblicalnutritionist.com)

- A website offering recipes, nutritional advice, and resources based on biblical dietary principles.

3. "Taste and See: Experiencing the Goodness of God with Our Five Senses" by Margaret Feinberg

- A book that combines culinary exploration with spiritual insights, featuring recipes and reflections on biblical foods.

Further Reading

1. "Eat and Be Satisfied: A Social History of Jewish Food" by John Cooper

- An in-depth look at the history and significance of food in Jewish culture and its biblical roots.

2. "The Spirit of Food: 34 Writers on Feasting and Fasting Toward God" edited by Leslie Leyland Fields

- A collection of essays that explore the spiritual dimensions of food, offering reflections and stories from various Christian writers.

3. "Food at the Time of the Bible: From Adam's Apple to the Last Supper" by Miriam Feinberg Vamosh

- A detailed exploration of the foods mentioned in the Bible, their historical context, and their significance.

By delving into these resources, readers can further enrich their understanding of biblical dietary practices and how they can be applied to enhance both physical health and spiritual well-being in modern life. These additional materials provide valuable insights, practical advice, and scholarly perspectives that complement the themes discussed in this book.

BIBLICAL VERSES USED THROUGHOUT THE BOOK

Chapter 1: Biblical Perspective on Food

- Leviticus 11 (Clean and Unclean Foods)

- Deuteronomy 14 (Clean and Unclean Foods)

Chapter 2: Healing Foods in the Old Testament

- Honey:

- Proverbs 24:13: "My son, eat thou honey because it is good; and the honeycomb, which is sweet to thy taste."

- Olive Oil:

- Isaiah 1:6: "From the sole of the foot even unto the head there is no soundness in it; but wounds, and bruises, and putrifying sores: they have not been closed, neither bound up, neither mollified with ointment."

- Figs:

- 2 Kings 20:7: "And Isaiah said, Take a lump of figs. And they took and laid it on the boil, and he recovered."

- Grapes and Wine:

- 1 Timothy 5:23: "Stop drinking only water, and use a little wine because of your stomach and your frequent illnesses."

- Pomegranates:

- Song of Solomon 4:3: "Thy lips are like a thread of scarlet, and thy speech is comely: thy temples are like a piece of a pomegranate within thy locks."

- Herbs and Spices:

- Psalm 51:7: "Cleanse me with hyssop, and I will be clean; wash me, and I will be whiter than snow."

- Isaiah 28:25,27: "When he hath made plain the face thereof, doth he not cast abroad the fitches, and scatter the cummin, and cast in the principal wheat and the appointed barley and the rie in their place? For the fitches are not threshed with a threshing instrument, neither is a cart wheel turned about upon the cummin; but the fitches are beaten out with a staff, and the cummin with a rod."

Chapter 3: Healing Foods in the New Testament
- Bread and Fish:

- Matthew 14:19-20: "And he directed the people to sit down on the grass. Taking the five loaves and the two fish and looking up to heaven, he gave thanks and broke the loaves. Then he gave them to the disciples, and the disciples gave them to the people. They all ate and were satisfied, and the disciples picked up twelve basketfuls of broken pieces that were left over."

- Mark 8:6-8: "He told the crowd to sit down on the ground. When he had taken the seven loaves and given thanks, he broke them and gave them to his disciples to distribute to the people, and they did so. They had a few small fish as well; he gave thanks for them also and told the disciples to distribute them. The people ate and were satisfied. Afterward, the disciples picked up seven basketfuls of broken pieces that were left over."

- Wine:

- John 2:9-10: "The master of the banquet tasted the water that had been turned into wine. He did not realize where it had come from, though the servants who had drawn the water knew. Then he called the bridegroom aside and said, 'Everyone brings out the choice wine first and then the cheaper wine after the guests have had too much to drink; but you have saved the best till now.'"

- Matthew 26:27-28: "Then he took a cup, and when he had given thanks, he gave it to them, saying, 'Drink from it, all of you. This is my blood of the covenant, which is poured out for many for the forgiveness of sins.'"

- Bread:

- John 6:35: "Then Jesus declared, 'I am the bread of life. Whoever comes to me will never go hungry, and whoever believes in me will never be thirsty.'"

- Luke 22:19: "And he took bread, gave thanks and broke it, and gave it to them, saying, 'This is my body given for you; do this in remembrance of me.'"

- Fish:

- John 21:9-13: "When they landed, they saw a fire of burning coals there with fish on it, and some bread. Jesus said to them, 'Bring some of the fish you have just caught.' So Simon Peter climbed back into the boat and dragged the net ashore. It was full of large fish, 153, but even with so many the net was not torn. Jesus said to them, 'Come and have breakfast.' None of the disciples dared ask him, 'Who are you?' They knew it was the Lord. Jesus came, took the bread and gave it to them, and did the same with the fish."

- Healing Miracles Involving Food:

- John 9:6-7: "After saying this, he spit on the ground, made some mud with the saliva, and put it on the man's eyes.

'Go,' he told him, 'wash in the Pool of Siloam' (this word means 'Sent'). So the man went and washed, and came home seeing."

Chapter 4: Herbs and Plants in Biblical Healing

- Hyssop:

- Exodus 12:22: "Take a bunch of hyssop, dip it into the blood in the basin and put some of the blood on the top and on both sides of the doorframe."

- Psalm 51:7: "Cleanse me with hyssop, and I will be clean; wash me, and I will be whiter than snow."

- Myrrh:

- Exodus 30:23-25: "Take the following fine spices: 500 shekels of liquid myrrh, half as much (that is, 250 shekels) of fragrant cinnamon, 250 shekels of fragrant calamus, 500 shekels of cassia—all according to the sanctuary shekel—and a hin of olive oil. Make these into a sacred anointing oil, a fragrant blend, the work of a perfumer. It will be the sacred anointing oil."

- Matthew 2:11: "On coming to the house, they saw the child with his mother Mary, and they bowed down and worshiped him. Then they opened their treasures and presented him with gifts of gold, frankincense and myrrh."

- John 19:39: "He was accompanied by Nicodemus, the man who earlier had visited Jesus at night. Nicodemus brought a mixture of myrrh and aloes, about seventy-five pounds."

- Frankincense:

- Exodus 30:34-36: "Then the Lord said to Moses, 'Take fragrant spices—gum resin, onycha and galbanum—and pure frankincense, all in equal amounts, and make a fragrant blend of incense, the work of a perfumer. It is to be salted and pure and sacred.'"

- Matthew 2:11: "On coming to the house, they saw the child with his mother Mary, and they bowed down and worshiped him. Then they opened their treasures and presented him with gifts of gold, frankincense and myrrh."

- Aloe:

- John 19:39-40: "Nicodemus brought a mixture of myrrh and aloes, about seventy-five pounds. Taking Jesus' body, the two of them wrapped it, with the spices, in strips of linen. This was in accordance with Jewish burial customs."

- Mint, Dill, and Cumin:

- Matthew 23:23: "Woe to you, teachers of the law and Pharisees, you hypocrites! You give a tenth of your spices—mint, dill and cumin. But you have neglected the more important matters of the law—justice, mercy and faithfulness. You should have practiced the latter, without neglecting the former."

- Balm of Gilead:

- Jeremiah 8:22: "Is there no balm in Gilead? Is there no physician there? Why then is there no healing for the wound of my people?"

- Mustard Seed:

- Matthew 17:20: "He replied, 'Because you have so little faith. Truly I tell you, if you have faith as small as a mustard seed, you can say to this mountain, 'Move from here to there,' and it will move. Nothing will be impossible for you.'"

Chapter 5: Dietary Wisdom and Health Benefits

- Clean and Unclean Foods:

- Leviticus 11

- Deuteronomy 14

- Whole, Natural Foods:

- Genesis 1:29: "Then God said, 'I give you every seed-bearing plant on the face of the whole earth and every tree that has fruit with seed in it. They will be yours for food.'"

- Moderation and Balanced Consumption:

- Proverbs 23:20-21: "Do not join those who drink too much wine or gorge themselves on meat, for drunkards and gluttons become poor, and drowsiness clothes them in rags."

- Regular Fasting and Its Benefits:

- Isaiah 58:6: "Is not this the kind of fasting I have chosen: to loose the chains of injustice and untie the cords of the yoke, to set the oppressed free and break every yoke?"

- Specific Healing Foods:

- Honey:

- Proverbs 24:13: "Eat honey, my son, for it is good; honey from the comb is sweet to your taste."

- Olive Oil:

- Ezekiel 16:13: "So you were adorned with gold and silver; your clothes were of fine linen and costly fabric and embroidered cloth. Your food was fine flour, honey, and olive oil."

Chapter 6: Recipes and Practical Applications
- No specific verses cited.

Chapter 7: Spiritual Dimensions of Food
- Bread:

- Exodus 16:4: "Then the Lord said to Moses, 'I will rain down bread from heaven for you. The people are to go out each day and gather enough for that day.'"

- John 6:35: "Then Jesus declared, 'I am the bread of life. Whoever comes to me will never go hungry, and whoever believes in me will never be thirsty.'"

- Matthew 26:26: "While they were eating, Jesus took bread, and when he had given thanks, he broke it and gave it to his disciples, saying, 'Take and eat; this is my body.'"

- Wine:

- Psalm 104:15: "Wine that gladdens human hearts, oil to make their faces shine, and bread that sustains their hearts."

- Matthew 26:27-28: "Then he took a cup, and when he had given thanks, he gave it to them, saying, 'Drink from it, all of you. This is my blood of the covenant, which is poured out for many for the forgiveness of sins.'"

- John 2:10: "Everyone brings out the choice wine first and then the cheaper wine after the guests have had too much to drink; but you have saved the best till now."

- Fruits:

- Deuteronomy 8:8: "A land with wheat and barley, vines and fig trees, pomegranates, olive oil and honey."

- Galatians 5:22-23: "But the fruit of the Spirit is love, joy, peace, forbearance, kindness, goodness, faithfulness, gentleness and self-control."

- Milk and Honey:

- Exodus 3:8: "So I have come down to rescue them from the hand of the Egyptians and to bring them up out of that land into a good and spacious land, a land flowing with milk and honey."

- 1 Peter 2:2: "Like newborn babies, crave pure spiritual milk, so that by it you may grow up in your salvation."

- Olive Oil:

- 1 Samuel 16:13: "So Samuel took the horn of oil and anointed him in the presence of his brothers, and from that day on the Spirit of the Lord came powerfully upon David."

- Luke 10:34: "He went to him and bandaged his wounds, pouring on oil and wine."

- 1 John 2:20: "But you have an anointing from the Holy One, and all of you know the truth."

- The Table:

- 1 Corinthians 10:16-17: "Is not the cup of thanksgiving for which we give thanks a participation in the blood of Christ? And is not the bread that we break a participation in the body of Christ? Because there is one loaf, we, who are many, are one body, for we all share the one loaf."

- Isaiah 25:6: "On this mountain the Lord Almighty will prepare a feast of rich food for all peoples, a banquet of aged wine—the best of meats and the finest of wines."

Chapter 8: Integrating Biblical Wisdom into Modern Life

- No specific verses cited.

This list compiles all the biblical verses referenced in the book, providing a comprehensive guide for further study and reflection on the spiritual and health-related principles of food in the Bible.